Alexis de Tocqueville's
Journey in Ireland

Alexis de Tocqueville's Journey in Ireland

July-August, 1835

Translated and edited
by Emmet Larkin

The Catholic University of America Press
Washington, D.C.

Publication of this book has been funded in part by a gift from the Associates of The Catholic University of America Press.

The paper used in this publication meets the minimum requirements of American National Standards for Information Science—Permanence of Paper for Printed Library Materials, ANSI Z39.48-1984.

∞

Frontispiece: Alexis de Tocqueville, 1805–1859, by Théodore Chasseriau. Versailles MV 7384. © Photo R.M.N.

Library of Congress Cataloging-in-Publication Data
Tocqueville, Alexis de, 1805–1859.
   Alexis de Tocqueville's journey in Ireland, July–August, 1835 / translated and edited by Emmet Larkin.
      p.   cm.
   Translated from French.
   Includes bibliographical references.
   1. Ireland—Description and travel—1801–1900. 2. Tocqueville, Alexis de, 1805–1859—Journeys—Ireland. I. Larkin, Emmet J., 1927– . II. Title.
DA975.T63   1990
914.150481—dc20   89-23851
ISBN 0-8132-0718-5 (alk. paper).
ISBN 0-8132-0719-3 (pbk. : alk. paper)

For Harold and Charlyne Orel

Contents

Contents

Contents

Part Five. Tuam–Mayo, 4–8 August, 1835

List of Illustrations

Preface

A number of years ago, while teaching my undergraduate survey course in Irish history at the University of Chicago, I decided to have my students read Tocqueville's notes of his journey to Ireland in July and August of 1835. The great difficulty at that time, however, was that J. P. Mayer's edition and translation of Tocqueville's *Journeys to England and Ireland* (1958) had long been out of print, and second-hand copies were difficult to find. I determined, therefore, to attempt a new translation and edition that would not only be suitable for undergraduate teaching but also contribute to a better understanding of Tocqueville's visit to Ireland, about which virtually nothing has been written. I have been assisted by so many friends and colleagues and received so much encouragement in this effort that it is hard to know where to begin in expressing my gratitude and thanks.

First of all, however, I must thank the Count and Countess d'Hérouville for their kind permission to see and quote the material presented from the Tocqueville papers. I am also deeply indebted to my colleague Professor François Furet, of the École des Hautes Études en Sciences Sociales and the University of Chicago and president of the commission for the publication of the complete works of Tocqueville, who arranged for me to see the letters and notes published in this volume. I must also acknowledge the kindness and help of Mme Françoise Melonio, secretary general of the commission for the publication of the complete works of Tocqueville, who placed at my disposal a complete photocopy of the manuscript of Tocqueville's notes in Ireland and typescript copies of the letters he wrote to his family from Ireland in July and August of 1835. I am also much indebted to Mlle Lise Queffélec, who is about to bring out a new edition of Tocqueville's journals of his travels in England and Ireland under the auspices of the commission for the publication of the complete works. Mlle Queffélec generously gave me a copy of her notes to her forthcoming edition, for which it is difficult to thank her enough.

I must also thank two of my oldest and dearest friends, Mme Janine Courtillon, of the Center of Research and Study for the Diffusion of French at St. Cloud, and Professor John W. Boyle, of the University of Guelph in Canada, for all their help in construing and translating some of the more difficult passages in Tocqueville's notes. In identifying the various people whom Tocqueville interviewed in Ireland I received considerable help from Mr. Gerald Lyne, Assistant Keeper of Manuscripts at the National Library of Ireland. I must also thank Mr. Patrick E. Dempsey, Senior Reference Librarian, Geography and Map Division at the Library of Congress, for all his help in establishing Tocqueville's actual route in Ireland. Mr. Vincent Giroud, curator of the General Collection of the Beinecke Rare Book and Manuscript Library at Yale University, was also very kind in facilitating my work in the Gustave de Beaumont papers. Finally, I must thank Mr. Blake Lisenby and Miss Julie Rogers, my graduate assistants at the University of Chicago. Mr. Lisenby helped prepare the index for this volume, and Miss Rogers not only helped prepare the index, but also typed the whole of the manuscript and then proofread and edited it. I alone, of course, am responsible for any of the errors that may yet be found in this volume.

The University of Chicago   EMMET LARKIN
December, 1989

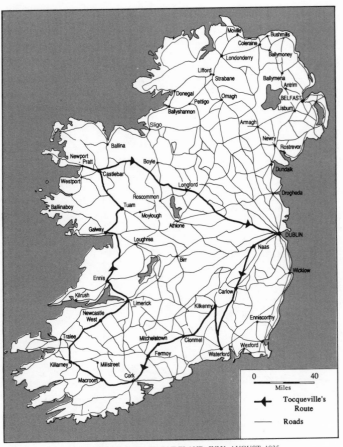

TOCQUEVILLE'S JOURNEY IN IRELAND, JULY–AUGUST, 1835

Irish roads in 1837, from the "Second Report of the Railway
Commissioners, Ireland, 1838."

Introduction

In July and August of 1835, Alexis de Tocqueville (1805–59) and his good friend Gustave de Beaumont (1802–66) spent about six weeks in Ireland. By the time the two young French noblemen had arrived in Ireland, however, they were already experienced travelers and observers with considerable scholarly and literary reputations. In 1831–32 they had spent nine months together in the United States and Canada, ostensibly on an official mission from the French government to investigate the American penal system, but actually to collect material for their projected study of the American political system. Some ten months after their return to France, in March 1833, they jointly published a study of the American penal system and its application to France, but the great work to emerge from their tour was Tocqueville's multi-volume study of *Democracy in America*, the first two volumes of which were published in January 1835. In the meantime, Beaumont had been writing a novel based on his American experience, *Marie, or Slavery in the United States*, which was also published in early 1835. In that spring of 1835, Tocqueville and Beaumont decided they would finally make the trip to the British Isles they had long been looking forward to.[1]

Tocqueville had, in fact, visited England in the summer of 1833 for about five weeks, to observe for himself the effect of the Reform Act of 1832 on what had become for him the central concern of his intellectual life since his visit to America: the great transition from an aristocratic to a democratic society then taking place in the western world. In England he was particularly concerned whether that transition could be made, as it had not been in France, without the trauma of a revolution. During his visit in 1833, he had come to the conclusion that the English people would be able to make the transition peacefully. After his second visit in 1835, he was even more convinced that the transition would be peaceful, but he was struck by two developments that might prove dangerous to the English democracy when it finally emerged full grown. The first was the increasing

1. André Jardin, *Alexis de Tocqueville* (Paris: Hachette littérature, 1984), p. 221.

I

centralization of the administration, and the second was the growth of a new aristocracy of wealth based on industry.[2] The problems posed for the survival of liberty in a democratic society by the newly emerged bureaucracy and plutocracy would be treated by Tocqueville in the subsequent volumes of his *Democracy in America*, published in 1840.

In any case, shortly after visiting the heartland of the new plutocracy in Birmingham and Manchester in late June 1835, Tocqueville and Beaumont crossed to Dublin via Liverpool on July 6 to spend some six weeks in Ireland. Their Irish trip considerably influenced the minds and work of both men. Before their trip, Tocqueville and Beaumont had apparently agreed to divide the English-speaking world between them. Tocqueville would write about America and Beaumont, England.[3] Beaumont, however, became so fascinated with Ireland in 1835 that he eventually decided to write about it instead of about England. He returned there again, during the summer of 1837, to finish collecting the necessary material for what was to become his most ambitious and enduring work, *Ireland: Social, Political and Religious*, which was published in 1839. Whether the 1835 agreement, to divide America and England between them, included Ireland is doubtful, but Tocqueville, apparently out of consideration for his friend's decision, never did anything more with his Irish notes. Whatever his intentions may have been in 1835, however, Tocqueville's Irish notes are both more detailed and literary than his English notes, and more interesting perhaps for what they reveal about him as a moralist as distinguished from a social scientist.

Some ten days after he arrived in Dublin Tocqueville wrote his father, Count Tocqueville, on July 16, reporting his initial experiences and impressions of Ireland.[4] "We are often frustrated," he explained, "as happened to us in Dublin, where we wasted four days of our time. Everyone for whom we had letters was in the country; after-

2. Ibid., pp. 225 ff.
3. Ibid., p. 229.
4. Tocqueville Papers, Tocqueville Archives, Chateau de Tocqueville, Tocqueville, France. (Hereafter cited as T.) Tocqueville to his father, July 16, 1835.

wards, they all wished to invite us to dine on the same day." "At last, however," he noted, "we were able to get going fairly well. But we discovered with regret that to understand this country well, it would be necessary to remain here not three weeks, but three months." "You cannot imagine," he further observed to his father, "what a complexity of miseries five centuries of oppression, civil disorders, and religious hostility have piled up on this poor people. It is a ghastly labyrinth, in which it would be difficult to try to find one's way, and of which we shall only catch a glimpse of the entrance." Indeed, Tocqueville had spent his first day in Dublin writing up his recent observations and thoughts about England, and did not date his first Irish note until July 9, when he ironically juxtaposed his descriptions of the poorhouse in Dublin and Trinity College. His most important contact in Dublin was Thomas Kelly, secretary to the Board of Commissioners of National Education, which administered the recently established Irish primary school system supported by the state. Kelly, who was a member of the Church of Ireland, apparently also introduced Tocqueville to a number of the clergy of the Established Church, who were especially interested in the education question.

Shortly after he interviewed Kelly on July 11, Tocqueville fell ill, and he was not well enough to continue his journey for more than a week.[5] All his discomfort in Dublin, however, was not just physical. "This country," he reported to his cousin, the Countess Grancey, on July 26, about a week after he left Dublin, "is divided in the most violent way between two parties which are altogether religious and political."[6] "On arriving in Dublin," he explained, "each of these two parties wanted to get hold of us, and make us see things through their *spectacles*. We acted like real Normans without ever saying either yes or no. They then stuffed us with letters of recommendation for the interior of the country and we left." The greater part of Tocqueville's notes of his three-week tour of the country (July 18–

5. Beaumont Papers. The Beinecke Rare Book and Manuscript Library, Yale University, New Haven, Connecticut. (Hereafter cited as B.) CX, Box 4, George Cornwall Lewis to Beaumont, July 20, 1835.

6. Alexis de Tocqueville, *Oeuvres Complètes* (Paris: Michel Lévy frères, 1864–67), Gustave de Beaumont, ed., VII, 126.

August 8) actually turn mainly on the two basic institutions responsible for effecting order in the countryside, the Roman Catholic Church and the courts of assize. The bulk of his notes, in fact, are based on either interviews or conversations: with Catholic bishops and priests, or with barristers and judges who were members of the various circuits of the courts of assize. His notes include as well accounts of the administration of justice at the assizes themselves. Curiously, though about half of the barristers on the various circuits were Catholic, Tocqueville appears to have interviewed only those who were Protestants. Whether this was by design, to secure some kind of balance in terms of the information he was collecting from bishops and priests, or by accident is difficult to say, but if the generally fortuitous way in which his trip to the South and West evolved is any indication, accident probably played the greater part.

"We left Dublin with many letters of recommendation for the interior of the country," Tocqueville reported to his mother, the Countess Tocqueville, from Kilkenny on July 24, a week after his departure, "but without any fixed plan. We went first to a little town near Dublin called Carlow. We had written the Catholic bishop there, who received us very well and invited us to dinner the same day."[7] "Chance would have it," he explained, "that this same day the archbishop of the province and four of his suffragan bishops were gathered at Carlow for a religious ceremony.[8] We dined with all these people

7. T., Tocqueville to his mother, July 24, 1835.
8. Tocqueville was not only mistaken about the "archbishop of the province" and the number of bishops present, but apparently also misinformed about their reason for being in Carlow. The archbishop, it appears, was that of Cashel, not of Dublin, and none of the *five* bishops present were suffragans of the archbishop of Cashel. Three western bishops of the province of Tuam (Patrick MacNicholas, bishop of Achonry, Patrick Burke, bishop of Elphin, and George J. P. Browne, bishop of Galway) were reported in the *Freeman's Journal* on July 17, 1835 as having arrived in Wexford town on a tour. The three western prelates were undoubtedly invited by Edward Nolan, the bishop of Kildare and Leighlin, to visit with him in Carlow on their tour, and he apparently also invited his good friends and near neighbors Michael Slattery, the archbishop of Cashel (Thurles), and William Kinsella, the bishop of Ossory (Kilkenny). Thurles and Kilkenny were respectively forty-five and twenty-four miles from Carlow. In counting the bishops present, Tocqueville apparently neglected to include his host, Edward Nolan, the bishop of Kildare and

and with several local parish priests. Everyone treated us wonderfully, and indeed each of these bishops invited us to come to see him in his diocese." "We reckoned on going to Cork, the great town of the South of Ireland," he added, "but we learned at Carlow that the assizes were being held at Waterford. We thought that this would be a good opportunity to form an opinion of the people who take part in these criminal procedures."

On July 21, therefore, Tocqueville and Beaumont set out for Waterford, where they attended the assizes for the next two days.[9] As they did not know anyone in Waterford, they apparently decided to write the presiding judge, Henry Joy, the chief baron, explaining that as members of the legal profession in France, and former magistrates in that system, they would appreciate being able to attend the assizes in Waterford.[10] The chief baron welcomed them and provided them with appropriate places in court; the barristers of the circuit adopted them as colleagues and extended them every hospitality. They even persuaded the two travelers to accompany them on July 24 to Kilkenny, where the assizes were to convene after Waterford. On arriving in Kilkenny, a distance of some thirty miles, Tocqueville recalled that it was the cathedral town of the Roman Catholic bishop of Ossory, and that he and Beaumont had met the bishop, William Kinsella, in company with the other prelates in Carlow, and Kinsella had then invited them to visit him. They therefore paid their respects to the bishop, who not only invited them to dinner that evening, but also asked them to dine with him again in company on Sunday, July 26.

The day Tocqueville was to dine again with the bishop was the same day he wrote the Countess Grancey his long letter already partially quoted. In this letter of July 26, Tocqueville not only attempted to explain how he found himself in Kilkenny, and why he felt obliged to leave it precipitously for Cork the following day, but

Leighlin, who, undoubtedly, had taken advantage of having the five prelates in Carlow to arrange a special religious ceremony in his cathedral on Sunday, July 20, and this was why Tocqueville thought the occasion was religious rather than social in its origins.

9. *Waterford Mail*, July 25, 1835.

10. T., Tocqueville to his mother, July 24, 1835.

also why crime in Ireland was as curious a phenomenon as it was a fascinating one.[11] "Would you, my dear cousin," Tocqueville requested, "please spread before you a map of Ireland, and try to locate a certain place called Kilkenny. It is a little town in the South of Ireland. This place, almost imperceptible on the map, has at this moment the advantage of possessing me. But its glory on this account will be very short-lived, for I am leaving tomorrow. I was attracted here by the *assizes*. No longer being able to judge or condemn anyone myself, I wanted to have the pleasure of seeing these things done by others." "Do you not recall," he asked, "the fable of the cat who had been changed into a woman and who found herself still chasing after the rats?"

> For a philosopher like me, moreover, there is nothing more curious than the assizes. These people commit the most singular crimes in the world. When they want to make a bargain with their neighbor, for example, guess how they go about it? They wait at night at the corner of a dark wood, with a bible in one hand and a pistol in the other, and they make him swear that he will sell his produce at half price. If the following morning he neglects to do it, they kill him. You are indeed aware that a man who violates an oath made on the Bible does not deserve any pardon. The main point is not to swear. For once it is done, by consent or by force, one is a ruined or a dead man.

"We would perhaps have remained longer in Kilkenny," Tocqueville added, "if the lawyers who follow the assizes had not thought of wanting to give us, my companion and me, as colleagues, a large dinner." "The prospect of a meal," he concluded amusingly, "with eighty persons, lasting six hours, washed down with at least twenty-five toasts and accompanied by two or three long speeches, in a word, a real English banquet, frightened us and caused us to flee."

By the time Tocqueville left Kilkenny the next morning, July 27, for Cork, and perhaps even before he had departed Dublin on July 18, he had apparently made up his mind about Ireland, for all his subsequent notes are really variations on three basic themes that had taken root in his mind since his arrival in Ireland. The first was

11. O.C., Beaumont, VII, 125–26.

the extraordinary poverty of the Irish people. The second was their enduring and implacable hatred for the Irish aristocracy, and the third was their deep and touching attachment to the church of their fathers. The appalling poverty, which Tocqueville first encountered on his visit to the Dublin poorhouse, was reaffirmed for him on his journey from Dublin to Carlow on July 19, and again two days later, on his way from there to Waterford. As he explained to the Countess Grancey, he had never seen anything like the misery of the poor, and to represent it literally boggled the mind. "I defy you, my dear cousin," he challenged her on July 26, "whatever efforts of the imagination you may make, to picture the misery of the population of this country. Every day we enter mud houses, covered with thatch, which do not contain a single piece of furniture, except a pot to cook the potatoes."[12] "I should have believed myself," he added, "returned to the huts of my friends, the Iroquois, if I saw a hole made to allow the smoke to escape. Here the smoke goes out by the door, which gives, according to my weak lights, a decided advantage to the architecture of the Iroquois."

"But I confess," Tocqueville confided, "what shocked me most in the beginning was to find a pig settled in the middle of the household. I infinitely respect pigs, but I cannot believe that Providence's view has been to make them the habitual companions of men. I will tell you, moreover, that from this association arises a considerable progress in the civilization of the pig."

> The Irish pig lends himself to the innocent games of the family of his host with a perfect charm. It is not rare to see the children of the house hanging on his tail. Far from becoming indignant with them, he gives evidence of his satisfaction by grunts full of gentleness; it is a charming spectacle, a very touching picture of rustic happiness.

"But when you are not used to it, as I said before," he admitted, "it shocks you. Those who are in a position to sleep with a pig are the well-off in Ireland. When he wallows complacently in the middle of the room, the owner of the house contemplates him with pride, and

12. Ibid., VII, 127–28.

I entered so completely into this sentiment that, when I want to seek shelter against the rain, I take particular care to choose a house where a pig is found." "When I catch sight only of men," Tocqueville finally observed ironically, concluding his amusing disquisition on the Irish pig, "I go elsewhere."

The second basic theme to emerge from Tocqueville's first three weeks in Ireland—the profound hatred of the people for their aristocracy—was only the other side of the coin of that aristocracy's scathing contempt for the people. While still in Dublin, Tocqueville was scandalized by the language of the aristocracy, which denominated the people as savages, reducing them to something less than human, and he attempted to analyze the patent failure of the Irish aristocracy to live up to its responsibilities by initiating a comparison with what for him had become that paragon of all aristocracies, the English. In writing to his father a few days before he left Dublin, Tocqueville was as yet able only to pose the question. "England and Ireland," he explained on July 16, "have the same language, the same laws, the same social structure, they are subject to the same government, and there are no [two] countries that present a more different appearance. Both have been for a long time, and are still in many respects, subject to a powerful aristocracy. This aristocracy has produced great wealth in England and frightful poverty in Ireland."[13] "In such a way," Tocqueville maintained, "if one wanted to pass judgment on *aristocracy in general*, by taking as a subject one of the two countries I have just mentioned, he would alternatively arrive at the most opposite conclusions, and, from any side, he would not encounter the truth, but two accidents." "The particular misfortune of this country," he pointed out, "has been to fall into the hands of an upper class who are different from the masses in race, in custom, and in religion and who nevertheless were invested with sovereign power, which they exercise under cover of the all-powerful protection of England." "Consequently, therefore," he concluded, "two nations entirely distinct on the same soil. The one rich, civilized, happy; the other poor,

13. T., Tocqueville to his father, July 16, 1835.

half savage, and overwhelmed by all the miseries by which God can strike man."

In his initial interviews and conversations with the Catholic bishops and clergy in Carlow, shortly after he left Dublin, Tocqueville learned that the profound chasm—social, economic, and political—between the aristocracy and people was widening rather than narrowing. These prelates maintained that the aristocracy cum landlords were exacerbating the problem by attempting to clear the people off the land, while the population was increasing and the attendant land hunger grew. On the evening of July 26, before they left Kilkenny for Cork and after they had returned from dinner with the bishop (who had denounced the landlords as a socially irresponsible class), Tocqueville and Beaumont decided that each would put his views of the relative merits of the English and Irish aristocracy in writing. In his short essay (episode 29), Tocqueville concluded that one could not generalize about the nature of aristocracy from these two histori- cal cases because the circumstances attending each were so different, but that the answer must rather be sought in an analysis of the virtues and vices most natural to aristocracy. Tocqueville's little essay on aristocracy, of course, has great relevance to any form of government, whether it be aristocracy, democracy, oligarchy, or even theocracy, for he is maintaining that the forms are neither good nor bad in themselves; rather, the circumstances determine whether the virtues, or vices, natural to the form are to predominate. In any case, there is little doubt that, in Tocqueville's view, the objective fact was that the Irish aristocracy had succumbed to all the vices inherent in the form and was from every point of view morally and politically bankrupt.

The third and final theme that Tocqueville had early made up his mind about in Ireland concerned the deep attachment of the Irish people to their church and its clergy. While in America, Tocqueville had come to appreciate the role of religion in a democracy, and more particularly the role of Catholicism. "I think," Tocqueville later wrote in *Democracy in America*, "that the Catholic religion has erroneously been looked upon as the natural enemy of democracy. Amongst the various sects of Christians, Catholicism seems to me, on the contrary, to be one of those which are most favourable to the equality of conditions."[14] "In France," Tocqueville then pointed out, "I had always seen the spirit of religion and the spirit of freedom pursuing courses diametrically opposed to each other; but in America I found that they were intimately united, and that they reigned in common over the same country." In attempting to discover the reason for this harmony between religion and liberty in America, Tocqueville put the question to a number of American priests, and they attributed the happy phenomenon mainly to the "separation of Church and State."[15] "I do not hesitate to affirm," Tocqueville added, "that during my stay in America, I did not meet with a single individual, of the clergy or laity, who was not of the same opinion on this point."

In Ireland, too, Tocqueville found the Catholic clergy, high and low, not only democrats to a man, but equally determined advocates of separation of church and state as well. The fundamental threat to that principle in Ireland in the early 1830s was the long-mooted proposal that the state should provide salaries for the Catholic clergy. In all his conversations with the Catholic clergy in Ireland, therefore, Tocqueville raised the question of their endowment by the state, and they uniformly declared themselves opposed to it because they thought it would prove ruinous to their relationship with their people.[16] This mutual regard and affection of priests and people for each other, Tocqueville came to realize, was the real key to basic social order in Ireland. The priest had become the natural leader of the people because, unlike their aristocracy, he had remained the incorruptible defender of their spiritual and material interests.

14. Alexis de Tocqueville, *Democracy in America* (London: Saunders & Otley, 1838), Henry Reeve, trans., II, 140.

15. Ibid., II, 150.

16. This was not the first time Tocqueville encountered this attitude on the part of the Catholic clergy. On his first trip to England in the summer of 1833, he had had a conversation (August 9) with a Catholic priest, Father Clarke, in Portsmouth, in which Clarke was adamantly opposed to any payment by the state of the Catholic clergy. Alexis de Tocqueville, *Oeuvres Complètes* (Paris: Gallimard, 1958), J. P. Mayer, ed., V, 24.

Tocqueville himself quickly acquired a real respect for this democratic priesthood, especially when he compared them to their Protestant counterparts. "At the first hotel," he explained to the Countess
Grancey on July 26, "we examined our letters, and we discovered they
had addressed nearly all of them to priests; nothing but *Reverends*, but
Reverends of different kinds. It would have been dangerous to make a
mistake about it. Some were Catholics and the others were Protestants."[17] "We continued on our way," he noted further, "and at each
place we went to see our two parish priests, who themselves never see
each other. We compare in the evening what they have told us."

> The Protestant minister is in general a holy man, whom God has
> not overwhelmed with work; he has twenty or so thousand
> francs [£800] income, forty parishioners, and a small gothic
> church, which is built at the top of the park. The Catholic priest
> has a small house, a much smaller dinner, five or six thousand
> parishioners who are dying of hunger, and share their last penny
> with him; and he fancies that this state of things is not the best
> possible one. He thinks that if the Protestant minister had a little
> less and the poor Catholic population a little more, society would
> gain by it, and he is amazed that five thousand Catholics are
> obliged to pay twenty thousand francs in taxes to support the
> religion of forty Protestants.

"But," Tocqueville concluded, ironically, "that is altogether revolutionary language, and that would not be put up with."

But behind Tocqueville's admiration for the Catholic clergy was
an even more profound respect, which he never made quite explicit
in his notes, for the quality of religion in Ireland. "One of the things
that strikes me most in Ireland," he explained to his good friend Louis
de Kergorlay shortly before he left Dublin for the country, "is seeing
how religious sentiment preserves its power here, without absorbing
and destroying every other driving force of human action."[18] "Nothing resembles less," he added, "what one sees in so many other
Catholic countries, where the majority do not think of religion, and
the minority think of nothing else."

17. O. C. Beaumont, VII, 126–27.
18. Ibid., VII, 129–30, Tocqueville to Kergorlay, July 1835.

I have always believed that there was danger even in the best of passions when they become ardent and exclusive. I do not except religious passion. . . . I would even put it first because, pushed to a certain point, so to speak, and more than any other, it makes everything else disappear, and creates the most useless or the most dangerous citizens in the name of morality and duty. I confess that I have always (secretly) regarded certain ascetic works, when something is seen in them other than a lesson intended for the monastic life, as supremely dangerous. To the degree that these works teach it, it is not healthy to separate from the world, from its interests, from its business, even from its pleasures, when they are honorable; and those who live, like the reader of such books, by acquiring private virtues can hardly fail to lose all that makes for public virtues.

"A certain lively concern for religious truths," Tocqueville maintained, "and not going to the point of the absorption of the mind in the other world, has always seemed to me, then, the state most consistent with human morality in all its forms. It is this milieu, it seems to me, that one finds more often in this country than among any other people that I know."

By the time Tocqueville left Kilkenny for Cork on the morning of July 27, therefore, he had acquired some very definite and fixed ideas about Ireland, and his experiences in the West of Ireland in the next two weeks did nothing to modify them. He and Beaumont arrived in Cork city (ninety-two miles distant) on the evening of July 27, and they apparently remained in Cork only one day before they set out on July 29 for Killarney (fifty-four miles). Undoubtedly, they spent so little time in Cork because they learned the assizes would not convene there for another two days, and that the cases on the calendar, moreover, were not only very few, but also not likely to be very interesting.[19] The day after they arrived in Killarney, July 30, they visited the celebrated Lakes and Muckross Abbey.[20] The following day, July 31, they continued on to Limerick (sixty-nine miles), where Tocqueville was expecting to find letters from his family and friends

19. *Cork Southern Reporter*, July 30, 1835.
20. B., CX, Box 4, July 30, 1835. See also Gustave de Beaumont, *L'Irlande Sociale, Politique et Religieuse* (Paris: C. Gosselin, 1839), I, 197–98.

in France.[21] After spending the night in Limerick, the two travelers set out the next morning, August 1, via Ennis, for Galway (sixty-five miles), where they arrived that evening in time for dinner with the barristers of the western circuit. "We remained three days," he reported to his father several days later on August 5, referring to Galway city, "in the town of which I speak. The assizes were held there and we attended some very curious trials."[22] "Galway, in itself," he observed, "is a remarkable town. The Catholics are by report in the proportion of a hundred to one there, which does not prevent them [the Protestants] from occupying the ancient cathedral, a large gothic edifice, in which they cannot fill the choir for the solemn ceremonies."

While in Galway attending the assizes and seeing the sights of that ancient town, Tocqueville and Beaumont decided to visit Newport-Pratt, near Castlebar in County Mayo, before returning to Dublin, in order to investigate the newspaper reports that the people there were actually dying of hunger. They accordingly set out from Galway for Castlebar (fifty-seven miles) on August 4, going by way of Tuam. They spent the next day, August 5, in Castlebar, and the following morning they left Castlebar for Newport-Pratt (eleven miles). During the whole of the month of July the parish priest of Newport-Pratt, James Hughes, had written numerous letters to the press, calling the attention of the public to the desperate plight of the peasantry in his neighborhood and pleading for help to relieve them.[23] On arriving in Newport-Pratt, the two travelers were both shocked and appalled by what they found.

"I wrote to my father from Castlebar," Tocqueville explained to his mother several days later on August 10, on his return to Dublin, "before undertaking one of the most curious excursions of this long trip. On the edges of the sea beside the great ocean is a population a little poorer than the rest of the Irish population, that is to say, they *actually* die of hunger there when the potatoes fail as they did last year."

21. T., Tocqueville to his mother, July 24, 1835.
22. T., Tocqueville to his father, August 5, 1835.
23. See *Freeman's Journal* (Dublin), July 8, 14, 21, 22, 25, 28, and 31, 1835 for the letters from Hughes.

We arrived there without knowing anyone, but we were taken to the home of the parish priest, who received us with open arms, fed and sheltered us for two days and accompanied us from cabin to cabin, thus causing us to see a collection of misery such as I did not imagine existed in this world. It is a frightening thing, I assure you, to see a whole population reduced to fasting like Trappists, and not being sure by fasting of surviving to the next harvest, which is still not expected for another ten days.[24]

Tocqueville and Beaumont returned to Castlebar from Newport-Pratt on the morning of August 8, a Saturday, and left immediately for Dublin (one hundred forty-four miles). They probably broke their journey that evening in Longford, which was about half way between Dublin and Castlebar.

They arrived in Dublin late Sunday evening, August 9, and the next morning they attended the opening meeting of the British Association for the Advancement of Science. Before they had left Dublin in July they had been invited to participate in the meetings, which were to continue the whole of the week. "You know," Tocqueville reported to his mother on August 10, "that we returned to Dublin to take part in a great scientific meeting, which will take place today and the days following. A very large number of distinguished men from Great Britain and some from the continent have come to Ireland for this opportunity."[25] "We have been this morning," he reported again that afternoon, "to the first meeting of the society I mentioned to you. We found there at least five hundred people; a great deal of noise and little work, as it happens generally in assemblies so numerous. But we ended by breaking up into committees, and thus, I hope, we shall occupy our time in a useful way." It is difficult to know exactly how Tocqueville and Beaumont occupied their time at the meetings because there is no notice of the two savants in either the official proceedings of the association or the newspaper accounts of the meetings.[26] There

24. T., Tocqueville to his mother, August 10, 1835.
25. Ibid.
26. *Report of the Fifth Meeting of the British Association for the Advancement of Science held at Dublin in 1835* (London, 1836). See also *Freeman's Journal*, August 11, 12, and 13 for an account of the proceedings of the association.

were, however, a number of reports and communications to the association that dealt with social statistics, and this may have been the aspect of the meetings that interested them the most. In any case, Beaumont remained in Dublin only until August 13, when he departed for Scotland. Tocqueville remained there until Sunday, August 16, when he crossed to Wales and made his way via Shrewsbury to Southampton,[27] where he embarked on August 20 or 21 for the isle of Guernsey and, after a very rough passage, sailed from there for Cherbourg and home.[28]

27. T., Tocqueville to his father, August 17, 1835.
28. O. C., Beaumont, VII, 131–32, Tocqueville to the Countess Grancey, August 7, 1835. This letter has been obviously misdated, and the correct date is more likely early September 1835.

Part One

Dublin, 6-18 July, 1835

Conversation between Mr. Senior and Mr. Revans, 7 June 1835.[1] Mr. Revans is the secretary of the Irish "Poor Law" Commission. He is a very intelligent young man. He belongs to the radical party.

S. To what do you principally attribute the poverty of Ireland?

R. To a landlord system that profits from the intense competition of laborers [for land] to exact from the farmers an excessive rent. From the moment a farmer begins to make a profit, the landlord raises the price of the lease. The result is that the farmer is afraid to make improvements, for fear of being taxed by his master for a much higher sum than his improvement would be worth to him, and he confines himself strictly to subsisting.*

*[This note and all the subsequent notes marked by asterisks are in the original manuscript and in Tocqueville's hand.] "This difficulty arises everywhere when the landlord and the farmer treat each other as strangers. But the evil is even greater with the system of large landlords."

1. Though this conversation took place in London more than a month before Tocqueville visited Ireland, it has been placed here because it serves as a very useful introduction to a number of important themes and ideas—poverty, morality, justice, sectarianism, and the insecurity of property—that Tocqueville became very concerned with during his visit to Ireland.

Nassau William Senior (1790–1864), classical economist and the first professor of political economy at Oxford, 1825–30, had been appointed in 1832 a member of the royal commission charged with inquiring into the administration and practical operation of the poor laws in England. The commission issued its report in 1834, and its recommendations provided the basis for the Poor Law Amendment Act, or the New Poor Law, in that same year. After Tocqueville's first visit to London in 1833, he and Senior became good friends and continued to correspond and visit until Tocqueville's death in 1859.

John Revans had been appointed secretary in 1832 to the same royal

S. Do you think that a good poor law would by its nature diminish this evil?[2]

R. Yes, by diminishing the competition of laborers and by putting the common man in a position to lay down, up to a certain point, the law to the proprietor of the soil.

S. Is the poverty as great as they say?

R. The poverty is horrible. The people live only on potatoes, and often they lack them.

S. The number of children is very great?

R. Yes. It has been observed that the poorer they were the more children they had. They believe they have nothing more to fear. They marry in despair, and try to forget the future.

S. What is the state of morality in Ireland?

R. This requires a great deal of explanation . . .[3] There is not a people more gentle than the Irish when the moment of anger has passed. They forget offenses easily. They are very hospitable. There is not an Irishman so poor that he does not share his last potato with someone who is in need. Crimes are very rare among them except theft, which occurs only in order to subsist. They steal things that can be immediately eaten. There is the good side. Here is the bad: there is not a

commission on the English poor laws on which Senior served. He was subsequently appointed secretary to the royal commission charged with inquiring into the condition of the poorer classes in Ireland, which made the first of its three reports in 1835. Revans was, therefore, one of the best informed men in England about social conditions in Ireland.

2. Ireland, unlike England, had never had a comprehensive poor law, and for several years before Tocqueville's visit, a considerable debate had ensued about whether a systematic measure for the relief of the Irish poor was necessary. The chief opponent to a poor law for Ireland was Daniel O'Connell, who had emerged as the leader of the Irish people in his successful campaign for Catholic Emancipation during the 1820s. O'Connell's objections were less economic than religious and moral. He felt that compulsory almsgiving was inimical to that charity enjoined by Scripture as a Christian duty.

3. All the ellipses in this text are in the original manuscript.

country where it is more difficult to obtain the truth from a man.*

S. The spirit of party is very strong in Ireland?

R. To a point that it would be almost impossible for you to conceive. It would take a foreigner ten years to understand the parties. Party spirit pervades everything, but particularly in the administration of justice. To tell the truth, there is no justice in Ireland. Nearly all the local magistrates are at open war with the population. Moreover, the population has no idea of public justice. In Ireland nearly all justice is extra-legal. Unless Englishmen are sent to serve as judges, it will remain the same there. The jury system is almost impracticable in Ireland.

S. Why do the Irish have such a great hatred for us?

R. Above all because we have always sustained the Orangemen, whom they consider as their oppressors.[4]

S. Of what is the Catholic Party composed?

R. Of nearly all the people. But very few wealthy and educated men are met with in this party, which has always been oppressed. That is a great misfortune.

S. Could an agriculturist who imported a large amount of capital into Ireland be sure of reaping the fruits of his industry?

R. No, the people are faced by evils too great, and kept

---

*This has been at all times the vice of the wretched and slaves.

4. The "Orange Society," which eventually became the "Orange Order," was founded in September 1795, in County Armagh, as the result of the bitter and violent sectarian strife between Catholics and Protestants in that county. The society was named after the Protestant Prince of Orange, later William III of England, who had defeated the Catholic James II at the battle of the Boyne in July 1690. Soon after the founding of the Orange Society, lodges were formed throughout the north of Ireland, and early in 1798 the Grand Lodge of Ireland was founded in Dublin. In time the Orange Order became national in scope, and the strongest and most effective promoter of Protestant ascendancy in Ireland as well as the bane of Irish Roman Catholics.

because of this in too great and continual a state of agitation for property to be secure there: the lack of security for property is the greatest evil in Ireland.

S. Do you not believe that this inferiority of the Irish to the English derives from a racial inferiority?

R. I do not know. But I am not disposed to believe it. In the districts where property is secure and where poverty reigns less, the peasant shows himself steady and progressive.

2

Conversation with Mr. W. Murphy.[5]

———————

Mr. Murphy, it is said, is the richest Catholic in Ireland. He is one of O'Connell's friends.

———————

Q. How many individuals do you estimate are unemployed in Ireland, although they are willing to work?

A. Two million.

Q. Do you think there should be a poor law?

A. The question seems to me to be so vast and so complicated that I confess that I have not made up my mind. I am afraid that a poor law would greatly increase the number of poor, and that the landlords would no longer get anything at all from their estates.

Q. What do you think then can be done?

A. I suppose, but this is only an opinion on my part, if one could settle a portion of the poor population of Ireland on

———————

5. This conversation, contrary to Tocqueville's usual practice, is undated, but it probably took place during Tocqueville's stay in Dublin from July 6 to July 18, 1835. William Murphy was a very wealthy Catholic merchant and head of the firm William and James Murphy and Co., located at Smithfield in Dublin.

land not yet cultivated but cultivable, this would be a great help.

Q. Is there much of this uncultivated but cultivable land?

A. Yes.

Q. But it is owned by somebody?

A. Yes, it forms part of vast properties, which were formerly acquired for nothing by rich individuals. Since they do not make any use of it themselves, Parliament could take it off their hands, even if that would entail paying them a certain price at the moment it would be cultivated.

Q. But do you believe the poor population of Ireland can be easily displaced and driven at will to the selected places, and when there, they would work profitably?

A. Most of the Irish poor ask only for work, and would work eagerly to pull themselves out of the frightful degree of poverty in which they live. As for displacing the population, nothing would be easier. The place of birth for such wretched creatures has not any value.

Q. What you have just said is the most complete proof that one could give of the wretchedness of the population. It is the last known degree of unhappiness that could force an *ignorant* and *moral* population to settle abroad. Is the improvidence among the Irish poor as great as it is said to be?

A. It is extreme. They marry at 16 or 18 years. Very often it is necessary to borrow to pay the priest. The more intolerable their poverty becomes, the more this spirit of improvidence seems to increase.

Q. Don't you think if the division of landed estates were greater, a larger number of people could live in greater comfort in the same space?

A. It would be extremely difficult to effect this division, even if the law of entail should not exist. The peasant is too poor to buy the land. The landlord would not find any buyers if he wanted to sell in small lots. He can only hope to get a good price by selling it as a whole.* Actually, the land is divided up among a small number of landlords; the whole Irish population, so to say, consists of very small [and] very poor tenant farmers, and laborers poorer still. It is impossible, for the present, to devise a way to change this order of things. At present, we prefer to do business with a large landlord rather than with a small one. The latter squeezes his tenants even more.

Q. So you do not have anyone who cultivates a field that belongs to him?

A. No.

3

Visit to the Poorhouse and the University. 9 July 1835.[6]

A vast edifice sustained annually by voluntary gifts. 1,800 to 2,000 paupers are received there during the day; they receive food, lodging, and when they are capable of it, work. They go to sleep where they can.

The sight inside. The most hideous and disgusting aspect of destitution. A very long room full of women and children whose infirmities or age prevent them from working. On the floor the paupers are lying down pell-mell like pigs in the mud

------

*It is the opposite in France. A difference that ought to be well considered.

6. The Dublin Poor House was founded by an act of the Irish Parliament in 1703, and was merged with the Foundling Hospital in 1771. The University of Dublin (Trinity College) was founded by Elizabeth I in 1592 to promote the interests of the Established Church of Ireland. The Corporation of Dublin contributed the site and buildings of the former Augustinian monastery of All Hallows, which had been granted to the city of Dublin at the dissolution of the Irish monasteries in the early 1540s. In 1835 Catholics made up about ten percent of the student body at Trinity College.

of their sty. One has difficulty not to step on a half-naked body.

In the left wing, a smaller room, full of old or crippled men. They are seated on wooden benches, all turned in the same direction, crowded together as in the pit of a theatre. They do not talk at all, they do not move, they look at nothing, they do not appear to be thinking. They neither expect, fear, nor hope for anything from life. I am mistaken, they are waiting for dinner, which is due in three hours. It is the only pleasure that is left to them, after which they will have nothing more than to die.

Further on are those who are able to work. They are seated on the damp earth. They have small mallets in their hands and are breaking stones. At the end of the day they receive a penny (two sous in France). They are the lucky ones.

On leaving there we came upon a small covered wheelbarrow pushed by two paupers. This wheelbarrow goes to the door of the houses of the rich; into it is thrown the remains of the meals, and this debris is brought to the poorhouse to make the soup.

From the poorhouse they took us to the university. An immense and magnificent garden kept up like that of a nobleman. A palace of granite, a superb church, a wonderful library. Lackeys in livery, 24 fellows, 70 [scholars]. Enormous revenues. Men of all religions are educated there. But only members of the Church of England can administer the establishment and receive its revenues.

This university was founded by Elizabeth with the estates confiscated from Catholics, the fathers of those whom we had just seen wallowing in their mud at the poorhouse! This establishment contains 1500 students. Very few belong to rich Irish families. Not only do the Irish nobility live abroad; not only do they spend abroad the money it produces, [but] they rear their children in England, for fear undoubtedly that the vague instinct of patriotism and youthful memories might bind them one day to Ireland.

If you wish to know what the spirit of conquest, religious hatred, combined with all the abuses of aristocracy without any of its advantages, can produce, come to Ireland.

4

11 July 1835 Mr. Kelly is a very intelligent Irish lawyer appointed by the government as permanent secretary of the *National Schools*.[7]

Mr. Wilson, minister of the Anglican Church (obviously one of the most moderate men of his order) was present at this interview and what follows is in effect the opinion of both these men.[8]

Q. Is it true that there are no small landowners in Ireland?

A. I do not believe that there is a single one.

Q. However, not all landed estates are entailed, and your entails, like those in England, are not perpetual.

A. It often happens that estates are sold. But then they are always sold as a unit. The landlord changes sometimes, but the estate is never divided. The idea of buying a small piece of

7. Thomas Frederick Kelly (born c. 1797) was appointed in 1831 the first secretary to the Board of Commissioners who administered the national system of education, and retired from that post in 1838. He was in religion a member of the Established Church of Ireland and by profession a barrister. He had been called to the bar in 1822 and later became a judge in the court of admiralty.

8. This may have been James Wilson (1780–1857), who took his M.A. degree in Trinity College in 1809, and his D.D. there in 1830. He became the Protestant bishop of Cork in 1848, and was imputed to be very liberal in religious matters. See *Freeman's Journal* (Dublin), January 9, 1857, for his obituary notice.

Page from Tocqueville's manuscript for 11 July 1835, an interview with Mssrs. Kelly and Wilson.

land never occurs to anyone, still less the idea of selling it. Besides, our civil laws render the transfer of landed estates from one hand to another expensive and difficult.

Q. Is it true that the estates are broken up into very small farms?

A. Yes, the system of small farms is universal.

Q. What is the cause of this state of things, so contrary to the interests of agriculture and to the well-being of the population?

A. There are several causes: The first is the poverty of those who wish to become tenant farmers. To work a large farm, one needs capital, and there are no Irish peasants who have that capital. The second is purely political. For a long time, the property qualification required to be an elector had been fixed very low, and the tenant-farmer elector always voted according to the interests of his landlord. The landlord there-fore had a very great political motive to break up his estate into as many small farms as possible in order to increase the number of electors who were loyal to him.

Q. But the raising of the property qualification to 10 pounds,[9] by diminishing the number of electors, and the hostile spirit established between the tenant farmers and the landlord, has duly put a stop to the second cause?

A. It has also resulted in that. Since the change in the elec-toral laws and the Emancipation Bill the landlords have busied themselves destroying the many small farms and consolidating them into larger ones. With this end in view they have evicted

9. In passing Catholic Emancipation in 1829, the Conservative government disenfranchised the forty-shilling freeholders in the counties, who numbered some 200,000 voters, and raised the property qualification for voting to ten-pound freeholders, reducing the electorate in the counties to about 16,000. The Reform Act of 1832 enfranchised the ten pound leaseholders in the counties, thus increasing the electorate to some 60,000 in that year.

all the small farmers who were in arrears in their rent (as nearly all of them were). This speedy eviction of a large part of the small cultivators has conspicuously increased poverty recently.

Q. Is it true the Irish landlords squeeze the agricultural population to the extent of almost depriving them of their means of living?

A. Yes. We have here all the evils of an aristocracy without any of its advantages. There is no moral tie between the poor and the rich. The difference of political opinion and religious belief, of race, [and in] the standard of living, render them strangers, one could almost say enemies. The rich Irish landlords extract from their estates all that they can yield. They profit by the competition created by the poverty, and when they have thus amassed immense sums of money, they go to spend them abroad.

Q. Why is the working population all drawn to agriculture, which increases competition in so extreme a way?

A. Because there are so very few industrial enterprises, [and] because the capital and the spirit of enterprise are wanting. Capital and the spirit of enterprise are wanting because the wealth and superior civilization of our English neighbors attract it all. Dublin had a flourishing cotton industry. Manchester has killed that business.

Q. According to what you tell me, although the agricultural population is poor, the land produces a great deal?

A. The yields are immense. There is no country where the price of farms is higher. But none of this wealth remains in the hands of the people. The Irishman raises beautiful crops, carries his harvest to the nearest port, puts it on board an English vessel, and returns home to subsist on potatoes. He rears cattle, sends them to London, and never eats meat.

Q. Do you think that a Poor Law would be a good thing for Ireland?

A. I believe so.

Q. But do you not think it is a dangerous remedy?

A. Yes. But Ireland happens to be in so exceptional a situation that one cannot apply general theories to it. It is necessary to find a way to compel the landlords to spend a portion of their money in the country. Do you know another way?

Q. There has been talk lately of demanding the repeal of the Union. Is it still an issue?

A. It is a dormant subject. O'Connell raised it. Other matters have taken up his attention. There the matter rests.

Q. What do you think of this question?

A. I think that the English will never consent to the repeal of the Union, and that there would be no chance of obtaining it short of force.

Q. But if the matter could be done peacefully would you think it desirable?

A. No. When we had an Irish Parliament, England looked on us as some sort of a foreign power, and rival; her jealousy was aroused, and as she had the wealth and the power she made us feel her superiority much more harshly than at present, when she looks on us as part of herself. When we had an Irish Parliament, the two races that divide this island were always facing one another, party spirit was more active, and the tyranny of the strongest party (the Orangemen) intolerable. The laws of that period are detestable.

Q. But don't you think that in our day things have changed? Today the Catholic party, so long suppressed, would not be long dominating in Parliament?

A. That would be a complete revolution. A tyranny of another kind no less great.

Q. Do you believe that England could hope to remain united with Ireland if the Irish Parliament were established?

A. No. I am convinced that the infallible consequence of such a measure would be the separation of Ireland, and all considered, I believe that the union of England and Ireland is necessary for the latter, and will become very profitable for her in time, if the English government, as everything gives promise, continues to take care of this country and sets itself up as a mediator between the two parties.

5

Mr. Kelly
Government

The kingdom is divided into parishes and counties like England. The administration is local here as in that country; in fact the administrative laws are almost the same, and if their effects are different, that appears to arise more from the state of civilization, the feelings of the inhabitants, and the particular political circumstances than from the nature of the laws themselves.

The lord lieutenant represents the king; he is the head of the armed forces, he has the right to grant pardons, he holds court. But he does not take part, I believe, in administration, except for the nomination of lords lieutenant of the counties, who, I believe nominate the justices of the peace. His influence is rather indirect. The political tendency, from what Messrs. Kelly and Wilson have told us, is to leave the lord lieutenant only the appearance of power and to concentrate all real power in the hands of the ministers in London. This tendency is natural and becomes perceptible in many other matters.

6

11 July 1835

Schools.   *Education*

We breakfasted this morning with two Anglican clergymen, Messrs. Smith and Todd, who told us much in criticism of the national schools.[10] They maintained that when the clergy of the Anglican church had some sort of a monopoly of primary education, because the annual grant from Parliament was placed in their hands or in those of a lay society entirely under their influence, they had, at that time, more Protestant and Catholic children mixed in the same schools and more hope of union between the two populations than under the influence of the present legislation, the object of which is to unite these two populations in the same schools. This is true enough, as will be seen, but I shall not draw the same conclusion as the reverend gentlemen.

The same day I went to dine with Mr. Kelly, the general superintendent of national schools, and I asked him to explain to me their history. He told me the following, which I find probable:

Until 1824 the Irish Catholic population seemed to be in a profound slumber. It submitted to its fate. In that period a great number of Catholic children frequented the schools of the Established Church. The teachers in these schools did not

10. Smith has proved impossible to identify, but Todd is undoubtedly James Henthorn Todd (1805–1869), Irish scholar and later regius professor of Hebrew at Trinity College, Dublin. Todd received his B.A. from Trinity College in 1825, and became a fellow and tutor in the college in 1831. He was very much opposed to the national system of education as established in 1831.

seek to exercise an influence on their beliefs; the parents at least did not fear this. About 1824, the Catholic population began to agitate. It claimed its political rights; the animosities became violent on both sides. The clergy of the Established Church wished to proselytize, the parents of the children became frightened. As the Catholic question advanced, and as the rights of the Catholic population were recognized in England, the situation worsened. In the eyes of all it became especially unfair that Parliament granted its support only to a sort of education that could not fail to excite the suspicions of the great majority of the inhabitants of the country, and particularly of the poorer classes for whom it was intended. In 1832 (I believe) Parliament was itself of this opinion and its *grant* was transferred to the new schools which the minister had created in the meantime.*

These schools were founded on the following plan:

A body of directors was founded in Dublin. This body was composed of two members of the Catholic clergy, two from the Established Church and two from the "Dissenters."† See the details in the official report.[11]

Mr. Kelly then gave us many of the practical details from which it seemed to us to follow:

1° That the number of schools and scholars was increasing rapidly.

2° That the "Anglicans" refuse to take part in this school system.

---

*Thus the national schools are not yet established by law. They exist only because the minister's recommendation has annually been approved by the legislature.

†Not all the details in this are exact. But I shall find them exactly in the reports.

11. The fact was that the original board of commissioners appointed to administer the national system of education consisted of seven members,

3° That the "Dissenters" took part only when the number of their children was large enough to enable them to form a school on their own.

4° That only the Catholics had accepted the idea eagerly. They zealously took part in its execution and drew great profit from it.

Thus, as nearly always happens to a weak government that wishes to proceed impartially in the midst of factions, after taking a stand on neutral ground, it is, in spite of itself, carried along in the current of a party.

In brief, the goal of the measure has not been achieved. If one had wished only to encourage education in general, it would have been sufficient to allow the different sects help in proportion to their needs. But it was wished to found schools that were non-sectarian and that united the members of all. And up to the present these schools seem to us to be frequented only by the members of one sect.

7

Mr. Kelly. 11 July 1835

Roads in Ireland

Mr. Kelly has explained to me in this way the system of roads in force in Ireland:

Q. Do you have many toll roads?

A. We have a certain number of them, but the majority of our roads are not toll ones at all.

Q. How are the latter maintained?

---

three belonging to the Church of Ireland, two Roman Catholics, and two Presbyterians.

A. Each year the sheriff of the county chooses among the large landlords 24 persons who are the grand jurors (*English system*). These 24 persons, or any number from them more than 12, meet twice a year (I believe), and after deciding what roads ought to be opened or repaired in the county, fix the amount of the tax that ought to be paid by the inhabitants. This tax can be levied only when the judge of the assize has *sanctioned* the expenditure.

Q. Are the roads built or maintained according to this system good?

A. They were for a long time very bad. Now most of them are good.

Q. Is this change the result of legislation or of some accidental causes?

A. Our roads were bad and they have become good under the influence of the same laws.

Q. To what do you attribute the change?

A. To public opinion, which turned around on this score, and which gave a new impetus to grand juries.

Q. You have told me that a part of your roads system were [*sic*] toll roads. How can you combine the two systems?

A. We do not find any difficulty in doing so. When we find that a stretch of road is traveled enough to defray easily the cost of its maintenance, Parliament is asked to discharge the county of the cost by making that road a "turn-pike." Nearly all the heavily used Irish roads are organized in this way.

Q. Do you entrust, as in England, the supervision of this work to a body of *trustees* nominated by Parliament who afterwards fill up themselves the vacancies?

A. Yes. And we have found, as I believe they have found in England, that this *self-elected* body, which is accountable to no one for their actions, is sometimes the occasion of great abuses.

Q. Which men are in general *trustees*?

A. Landlords in the neighborhood of the road. They do not receive any emolument, but they very willingly undertake to fulfill these functions, which occupies their leisure time and gives them a certain importance in their district. When I spoke earlier of the abuses that result from the present system of *trustees*, I do not wish to say that they are accused of putting the money for the roads in their own pockets, but there are indirect misappropriations, such as sinecures created to oblige an individual, certain work granted to one individual rather than to another, although he will not do it as cheaply. . . .

8

Kingstown Regatta (11 July 1835)

Entertainment given to Lord Lieutenant and Lady Mulgrave by the railway company.[12] A fully royal ceremony for the viceroy. A great luncheon is given in his honor at Kingstown. Consists in large part evidently of Irishmen who are not Orangemen. Toast to the *Resident noblemen*! received with acclamation. A singular toast that can be understood only after one has lived some time in this country.

12. Earl of Mulgrave, Sir Constantine Henry Phipps, (1797–1863). Educated at Harrow and Trinity College, Cambridge, M.A. 1818; M.P. Scarborough, 1818, Higham Ferrars, 1822, Malton, 1826, and a supporter of Parliamentary reform; governor of Jamaica, 1832–34; lord privy seal with a seat in the cabinet, 1834; lord lieutenant of Ireland, 1835–39. See *Freeman's Journal* (Dublin), July 13, 1835, for a report on the regatta and Lord and Lady Mulgrave's attendance at it.

Part Two

Carlow-Waterford,
19-23 July, 1835

9

Appearance of the country from Dublin to Carlow.

Pretty country. Land very fertile. Beautiful road. Toll gates far apart. From time to time some very beautiful parks and rather pretty Catholic churches. Most of the dwellings of the country very poor looking. A very large number of them wretched to the last degree. Walls of mud, roofs of thatch, one room. No chimney, smoke goes out the door. The pig lies in the middle of the house. It is Sunday. Yet the population looks very wretched. Many wear clothes with holes or much patched. Most of them are bare-headed and bare-foot.

19 July 1835

10

20 *July 1835* (Carlow)

Conversation with Msgr. Nolan, bishop of Carlow.[13] He is a man of middle age who expresses himself with spirit and style.

It is above all necessary to consider this conversation (as all the others) as indicating the state of feelings more than the naked truth.

Q. Are landed estates divided up in County Carlow?

A. No. No more so than in the rest of Ireland. County Carlow belongs almost entirely to two families. These two families are not among the richest in Ireland. The duke of

13. Tocqueville is referring here to Edward Nolan, the bishop of Kildare and Leighlin. Carlow is the cathedral town of the diocese of Kildare and Leighlin. Nolan had succeeded to the see in August 1834.

Leinster, for example, has landed estates in the neighboring counties worth 70,000 pounds sterling in rents.

Q. Are there many "middlemen" in County Carlow, that is to say, men who take a lease of a portion of the estates of the great landlords, of whom you speak, to sublet it to others?.

A. Yes. The two great families of whom I speak have given very long leases for the greatest part of their estates. The foremost tenant farmers, who are themselves very rich people, have sublet to others, and the latter to others.* In County Carlow, most of the estates serve the needs of four classes of individuals. You may imagine the last is wretched.

Q. Is there great discord between the people and the landlords?

A. An extreme discord, and which seems to be increasing rather than decreasing. Since the last election, when the Catholic candidates won, the two great families of which I was speaking introduced a new system of cultivation. They have evicted nearly all their small farmers. One alone evicted 150 families. They have enlarged their farms and introduced Protestant farmers. It is so in most of the counties. This enlargement of farms is a great evil. It diminishes the number of hands needed on the land, and as the large mass of the population in Ireland has no *other opportunity* than the land, it causes frightful poverty.

Q. So, in your opinion the poverty is increasing?

A. Without a doubt. The population is increasing rapidly and the means of employing it are decreasing. It is a frightful state of society. For my part, I believe the adoption of "poor laws" indispensable. The natural link that should unite the upper and lower classes is destroyed. The latter have nothing to expect from the former if the law does not come to their aid.

---

*Clear advantage here of the laws that divide up landed estates.

Q. What is, in your opinion, the morality of the poor?

A. They have many good qualities mixed with the faults that poverty brings. They are gentle, polite, hospitable. An English population would not endure for a week the state of poverty in which they are obliged to live. But when the occasion of drinking to excess presents itself they do not know how to resist it. Then they become turbulent and often violent and disorderly. Theft is very rare among them. Their morals properly speaking are very pure. Acts of violence are rather frequent, but they all derive from drunkenness or political passions.

Q. Have you had in this county many "Whiteboys" or "Whitefeet" (as they commonly call themselves now)?[14]

A. Few in this county. Many, two years ago, in the surrounding counties. I remember at that time Mr. X (I have forgotten his name), a neighboring priest, found a gang of "Whitefeet." He met with them and he reproached them severely. Their leader, who was a very intelligent man, replied almost word for word as follows (which he repeated to me immediately): The law does nothing for us, we must save ourselves. We are in possession of a little bit of land which is necessary to our and our families' survival. They chase us from it, to whom do you wish we should address ourselves ? We ask for work at 8 pence a day, we are refused—to whom do you want us to address ourselves? Emancipation has done nothing for us. Mr. O'Connell and the rich Catholics go to Parliament. We are starving to death just the same.

Two years ago, I was summoned to visit in prison a man who had killed the agent of a rich landlord. This agent wanted

14. The term "Whiteboys" was the generic name given to the agrarian secret societies that were endemic in Ireland from 1761 down to the Great Famine of 1847. These societies had been particularly active during the agitation against the tithe imposed by the Established Church of Ireland during the early 1830s.

to change the method of cultivation and to achieve this he evicted the small farmers and destroyed their houses. One of them had a sick wife and asked for a respite. The agent had the sick woman brought outside the house in the open air and destroyed her house before her eyes. Some days after, he was murdered by the man who was speaking to me, [and] who was not personally interested in any way in the act that I relate, but who acted out of vengeance for that deed. These crimes are frightful. But what a horrible state of society!

Q. Do you think that the Irish Catholic clergy [should] receive an allowance from the English government?

A. No. The Catholic clergy would then lose their influence over the people. I do not know what it is proper to do in other countries, but I do not doubt that in Ireland the clergy would lose a great deal by the change and that religion itself would suffer by it. There exists between the clergy and people of this country an unbelievable union.

II

Carlow 20 July 1835

Conversation with Mr. Fitzgerald, the president of the Catholic college at Carlow.[15] Mr. F. is an amiable old man. Catholic and democratic passions appear more openly with him than with the bishop.

Q. Are the ills suffered by the people very great?

15. Andrew Fitzgerald, O.P. (1763–1843). A native of Kilkenny, Fitzgerald was educated in the College of Kilkenny, and at the age of sixteen he entered Louvain University, where he joined the order of St. Dominic. He did his philosophy and theology at Louvain and finished his studies at Corpo Santo in Lisbon before returning to Ireland in 1792. In 1800 he was appointed professor of classics in Carlow College, and in 1814 he became president of

A. Frightful. You see it yourself. The people are treated as conquered by the landlords, and in fact the latter occupy the estates that have been confiscated from these same Catholics, who are dying of hunger. The upper classes are to blame for all the ills of Ireland.

Q. Is it true that the discord between the upper and lower classes is increasing?

A. Yes. As long as the upper classes saw the Catholics as slaves, submitting to their fate with resignation, they did not treat them violently. But since political rights have been granted to the Catholic population, and they wish to exercise them, they persecute them as much as they can and seek to root them out of their lands in order to put Protestant farmers in their place.

Q. Is it true that the people have not the least confidence in justice?

A. Not the least. The poor believe themselves in some way outside the law.

Q. The clergy, it is said, are very united with the people.

A. Intimately. It ought to be so in all countries. When I was in France ten years ago, and I saw the absurd way in which the French clergy tried to influence the population, I did not doubt that a new revolution was drawing near. The French priests appeared to me far from enlightened and far from wise. Their plantation of mission crosses, among other things, appeared to me a great folly in the interests of religion.[16]

---

that college. In 1832 Fitzgerald was arrested and imprisoned for his refusal to pay the tithe.

16. Fitzgerald is referring here to the Missions of France, founded by Abbé Rauzan in 1814 to rechristianize France. The missions were conducted by the priests of various religious orders, who by their passionate preaching attempted to reconvert those who had become lukewarm or indifferent to religion. The preachers were particularly adept at invoking the punishments of hell and staging spectacular ceremonies, such as collective communions, mass confessions, processions to the tune of martial music, and acts of atone-

Q. Would you like a subvention from the state?

A. No. Certainly not. And in general we are very opposed to any tie between church and state.

Q. How do you choose your bishops?

A. At each vacancy the parish priests of the diocese meet. They nominate three candidates from among whom the pope chooses. In general he chooses the first.

Q. From which class, in general, are your priests taken?

A. From the tenant-farming class.

Q. How much is a parish worth?

A. About 300 pounds sterling.

Q. And the bishoprics?

A. The best paid, £1000. The least, like that of Carlow, 500.

Q. How are ecclesiastics paid?

A. They are remunerated for most of the activities of their ministry. Furthermore, there is a collection made for them twice a year.

Q. And the bishops?

A. The pay of the bishops consists of the income of a parish, and in addition a certain sum that each parish priest is required to pay them.

Q. Do the poor contribute more, all things considered, than the rich?

---

ment for the outrages committed during the Terror in the recent Revolution. The most spectacular ceremony of all, and the most controversial, was that which closed the mission. After a long procession miming Christ's road to Calvary, in which the cross was carried by volunteers in relay, and at which all the local authorities attended, a gigantic cross was set up in the most prominent place in the town to the cheers of the multitude. Between 1815 and 1830, about fifteen hundred missions were conducted, of which some one hundred and thirty took place in the larger towns. These missions were not without their political implication, and especially after 1821, when the Liberals began to organize an opposition to them. The result was that the missions were often the occasion of brawls and riots, and the more moderate Royalists began to look on them with a good deal less favor. I am much indebted to Mlle Lise Queffélec for the substance of this footnote.

A. I think so.

Q. How much did your cathedral in Carlow, which seems to me quite new, cost?

A. 30,000 pounds sterling. This money was raised all over Ireland.

Q. The college over which you preside, which contains 180 students, as many secular as ecclesiastical, is it entirely supported by voluntary contributions?

A. Entirely.

Q. Are there many rich Catholics?

A. Many have considerable fortunes in personal property. But, all the landed estates are in the hands of Protestants.

Q. Is the dissension between Protestants and Catholics so great as to be harmful to social relations?

A. The Catholics and Protestants of Carlow avoid seeing and speaking to each other. The inn where you lodge is kept by Protestants. I am sure that on seeing me enter there to visit you, they were extremely surprised.

Q. Your age enables you to make comparisons. Do you think the poverty of the population increasing or decreasing?

A. I believe that it is increasing.

Q. You have lived in the times of oppression; was it great?

A. Terrible. Would you believe, sir, that in my youth a Catholic could not become a schoolmaster. It was necessary to leave one's children without education or send them to a Protestant school.

Q. Does the population now show an enthusiasm for education?

A. A very great enthusiasm. There are parents who beg so that their children can go to school. But this is a recent fact. The rising generation will be infinitely better educated than the present one.

Q. Do the people pay the tithe.[17]

A. No, they have stopped paying it and they will never pay it now. If the tithe is removed from the tenant farmer and placed on the landlord, and if, as a consequence of this new order of things, the landlord should wish to raise the rent, I am convinced that there will be also resistance among the poor whose attention has been awakened on this point. Is it not revolting that the Protestant clergy, which does hardly anything for the people, should enrich itself to their detriment and apply to its own use the tithes, which have been established not only to provide for the needs of the priest, but also for those of the poor and for public education?

12

20 July 1835
Dinner with the bishop of Carlow

There was an archbishop, four bishops, and several priests there.[18] All these gentlemen had very good bearing. The meal was served decently but without ostentation. The dinner was good but not elaborate. These ecclesiastics drank very little. They all appeared to be gentlemen.

17. Before 1735 all Irish land under cultivation, whether tillage or pasture, was subject to the payment of the tithe. In 1735, the Irish Parliament passed a resolution against the payment of the tithe on pasture land. Though the resolution was not legally binding, beginning in 1735 the tithe was collected only on land under tillage. In 1830, an agitation against the payment of the tithe broke out in County Carlow and soon spread to other parts of the country; over the next several years, the efforts (on the part of those by law entitled to the tithe) to collect it by distraining the property of those who refused to pay it resulted in the large-scale resistance and the considerable bloodshed that became popularly known as the "tithe war."

18. See Introduction, nn. 7–8.

The conversation turned on the state of the country and politics. The sentiments expressed were extremely democratic. Contempt and hatred for the great landlords. Love of the people, confidence in them. Bitter memories of past oppression. A certain exultation at present on approaching victory. A profound hatred of the Protestants and, above all, of their clergy. Little apparent impartiality. Clearly as much the heads of a party as the representatives of the church.

13

Cause of the present distress

The archbishop of Munster,[19] whom I sat beside today (20 July 1835) at dinner, explained to me in the following way why the wretchedness of the poor has increased for several years. Three causes:

1° Under the old election law the farmers who held their leases on the life of a man (a very frequent kind of risky lease, which lasts as long as the several individuals so designated live) were electors, while the farmers furnished with ordinary leases were not. The result of this was that the landlords, in order to increase the number of the electors dependent on them, divided their estates in very small parts and leased them in this way, having care to base the lease on the life of an old man so as to have the elector always dependent on them. The new election law has destroyed this class of electors and has fixed the cost of the franchise so high that very few of them can attain it. The landlords

19. In identifying the bishops, Tocqueville did not use their correct episcopal titles, but designated their jurisdictions in civil rather than in ecclesiastical terms. In identifying the bishop of Kildare and Leighlin, for example, he called him the bishop of Carlow, and here he identifies Michael Slattery, the archbishop of Cashel, as the archbishop of Munster.

then hasten to evict these small farmers, which has thrown a great number of families on the road.

2° The division of the country into small farms not being, politically speaking, useful any more, the landlords have begun to think that the large farmers were, economically speaking, preferable, [and] they have constantly strained, from the point of view of political economy, to destroy the little farms and make large ones of them, which again throws a large number of families on the road.

3° The *evictions* for political enmity and vengeance throughout the country, where it is possible to have Protestant farmers, the tendency of the landlords is to evict the Catholic population, which again throws daily a large number of families on the road.

14

20 July 1835 Carlow

Irish Clergy

There exists an unbelievable union between the Irish clergy and the Catholic population. But that is not only because the clergy are paid by the people, but also because all the upper classes are Protestants and enemies.

The clergy, rebuffed by high society, leans entirely towards the lower classes. They have the same instincts, the same interests, the same passions as the people. A state of affairs altogether particular to Ireland, and which it is necessary to examine well when one speaks of the advantages of the system of voluntary remuneration.

In the streets of Carlow, I noticed that the people greeted with great respect all the priests who passed.

I was at dinner today with an archbishop, four bishops, and several Irish parish priests. All were agreed that it was necessary at all costs to avoid being paid by the government. They admitted however that there were some individuals in the body who would like nothing better.

Carlow 20 July 1835

15

The Irish aristocracy—judged by themselves and by all parties

---

I have not yet met a man in Ireland, to whatever party he belonged, who did not acknowledge, with more or less bitterness, that the aristocracy had governed the country very badly. The English say it openly, the Orangemen do not deny it, the Catholics shout it at the top of their voices.

I find that the language of the aristocracy proves it more than all the rest.

All the rich Protestants that I saw in Dublin speak of the Catholic population only with an extraordinary hatred and contempt. They are, to all intents, savages incapable of recognizing a kindness, fanatics led into every disorder by their priests.

Now, these same people who hold such language, are those who have held, and still hold in part, the whole government of the country. How to expect that people animated by such feelings and imbued with such opinions (rightly or wrongly, I do not know) can treat with kindness, trust, or even justice, those about whom they express themselves so?

Carlow 20 July 1835

16

Schools

At Carlow *the national school* for girls is conducted in a convent and by the nuns. The Catholic priests appear extremely pleased with these schools, a further proof that they are entirely used by the Catholic party.

Carlow. 20 July 1835

The enthusiasm of the Catholic population for learning. A new development attested by the archbishop of Munster and the president of the College.

Carlow 21 July

17

Journey from Carlow to Waterford

General appearance of the country. 21 July 1835

We go on to County Kilkenny. From Carlow to Thomastown the appearance seems to us to become a little less wretched. Nearly all the houses have good chimneys. Some seem new and built on a slightly better plan. Sometimes the pig has a sty apart. Fewer people bare-foot and bare-headed than in the neighborhood of Dublin. From Thomastown to Waterford the appearance of the county again becomes very wretched. Many houses in ruins.

From Carlow to Waterford undulating country. Rather high hills. Views very extensive. No woods. Not many hedges. Fields surrounded by stone walls, which gives them a sad appearance. Few villages, but many scattered cabins. No churches. Near Thomastown the ruins of a monastery.[20] The ground remains consecrated in the eyes of the inhabitants, for around these ruined walls they still bury their dead. A touching scene of the attachment of this poor population to its beliefs. No factories. No passable dwellings. We travel alongside two or three magnificent parks, very well kept. All the rest only marks out the life of the poor. In the villages no small tradesmen, or only those nearly as wretched as the peasants themselves. No sign of activity except the land. Farm laborers in rags. There is an upper class and a lower class. The middle class evidently does not exist; or at least it is confined to the towns as in the middle ages.

In Thomastown I ask my host what is the average price of leases in the neighborhood. He replies 4 pounds sterling per acre. He complains of the poverty of the inhabitants and the hardness of the landlords, who profit from the destitution of the people to extract from them immense profits. I ask him if there are still "Whiteboys" or "Whitefeet." He replies no; that now the country is very quiet.

At a village between Thomastown and Waterford I ask a peasant what is the usual price of farms. He tells me 2 pounds sterling. I remarked on the poverty of the inhabitants and the repulsive appearance of the houses. Smiling, he replies that it is the same everywhere in Ireland. I ask him if there are great landlords in the neighborhood. He replies there are several, but like the others they live in England, where they spend the

20. Tocqueville is referring here to Jerpoint Abbey, a Cistercian monastery founded in 1157. In 1541, the monastery was suppressed by Henry VIII and its land granted to James Butler, the ninth earl of Ormonde.

country's money. Asked if there would not be a way to compel them to remain. Answer: yes, by taxing the absentees.

Asked if there is a Catholic church. Answer yes, a mile away. The parish is very large. A parish priest and two curates. Asked how many Protestants in the parish. Answer three. Where is the Protestant minister? He lives in Waterford. Do they still pay the tithe? No, they stopped paying it three years ago. How much did the tithe amount to? 10 shillings per acre of wheat or potatoes. 8 shillings per acre of barley. Meadows were exempt.

18

Persecutions

Mr. Plunkett, a Dublin lawyer, told me today (22 July 1835) it is only since 1782 that the Catholics can own land.[21] Before that time the law prevented it. One should not be surprised therefore that the Irish population is so completely excluded from the land and that it is so little divided up. *Waterford*

19

Waterford Assizes. 22 and 23 July 1835[22]

Catholic defends tolerance and liberty.
Protestant attacks the enlightenment and a Tory.

21. This may be John Span Plunkett (1793–1871), second son of William Conygham Plunkett, the first Baron Plunkett, and lord chancellor of Ireland, who became Crown prosecutor on the Munster circuit and an assistant barrister for County Meath.

22. See *Waterford Mail*, July 25, 1835, and *The Constitution; or Cork Advertiser*, July 25, 1835, for accounts of the Waterford Assizes.

Tocqueville was not consistent in titling and dating his episodes. Sometimes he would have a covering title page with the apropriate title and date for an

County Waterford Assizes. 22 and 23 July 1835

16 cases of murder. All these affairs turned out to be volun tary manslaughter or negligent homicide. But in all these af fairs, I believe, a man had been killed. These assizes gave us the very clear impression that the lower classes of this county are very prone to quarreling and fighting; that nearly every village forms a kind of faction, which has a soubriquet. Fac tions that began nobody knows when and continue nobody knows why, without taking on any political significance. When men of these different factions meet each other at a fair, a wedding, or elsewhere, it is rare they do not come to blows for the sole pleasure of the excitement that a fight gives. These quarrels very often end in the death of someone. In general a man's life here seems of very little value. This is the result of our observations and also of all that we hear.

In a civil action heard before the same court, a "*gentleman*" was accused of having struck another with a cane. The latter cited him before the court and to excuse this *legal* way of acting against accepted prejudices, his lawyer said: What would happen, gentlemen, if the *barbarous and violent state in which the lower classes of this country are unhappily placed* spread to the upper classes. If men of the upper classes resorted at every turn to physical force like the people, would not civilization soon disappear in this country? This was evidently everybody's opinion.*

---

*This disposition of the Irish to quarrels and violence is so well known that the law regards these offenses in a much more unfortunate light in Ireland than in England, and shows much less tolerance for involuntary homicide.

---

episode, and then he would also title and date it again on the page where he began the episode proper. In the interest of reproducing a faithful account of Tocqueville's text, I have, therefore, included all the titles and dates in the manuscript, even when they appear to result in a redundancy.

Most of the accused and the[23] [. . . The jurors are called and
take the oath. The first witness is called at once (the others
remain present in the court). The *prosecutor for the Crown*,
that is to say the lawyer fulfilling the function of the public
prosecutor, examines the witness. The lawyer for the accused
undertakes the *cross-examination*. If the judge thinks that a
question by one or the other is *improper*, he prevents it from
being asked. The witness being heard, the judge, who has
taken notes, sums up in a way in which he often undisguisedly
reveals his opinion to the jury. After which the jury retires.
They give their verdict. If it is guilty, the judge pronounces the
sentence immediately, as is the case in an acquittal. During the
whole course of the trial the accused appears to be a spectator.
He says nothing. He is asked nothing. He speaks if he wants
to, but no one asks him to speak.

My general impression is that English [*sic*] procedure is
much more expeditious than ours; that it often excludes in-
criminating evidence; that the system of *examination and
cross-examination*, without counsel's speech in the petty cases,
is better than ours; that the position of the accused would be
infinitely better than with us, if under the magistrate's robe
were not found an English Protestant, and if the political and
religious passions did not often do violence to the impartiality
of the judge. . . .]

At the Waterford Assizes the Crown counsel was a Dublin
lawyer who followed the circuit; although momentarily exer-
cising the functions of public prosecutor, he had not lost his

23. There is a folio page missing here in the manuscript, and recourse
therefore has been had to the text first published by Beaumont in 1865
of Tocqueville's *Journey to Ireland*. Unfortunately, the selection made by
Beaumont from the original manuscript does not include the whole of the
missing folio page, and hence the truncated nature of the presentation and the
necessity for ellipses at the beginning and the end of the extract. See Alexis de
Tocqueville, *Oeuvres Complètes*, Gustave de Beaumont, ed., VIII, 393.

character as a barrister. After having conducted a criminal case against an accused, he changed sides and pleaded before the same judge as lawyer in a civil matter. He even went so far, led on by his zeal as an advocate, to be astonished that the adversary of his client had not had recourse to arms rather than appeal to the tribunal. What made this even more singular in his mouth was that five minutes before, he had been prosecuting five or six peasants for having acted as he now appeared to believe it was necessary to act. This inconsistency was raised by the judge and the lawyer for the other side.

The jury changes only when there are challenges. Otherwise the first jurors chosen sat on all the cases of the day, which saved a great deal of time.

All the procedures of the two courts of justice that make the circuit are conducted with a rapidity unknown in France. The administrative procedures, the criminal and civil affairs are mixed in such a way as never to lose a moment. The grand jury is in session at the same time as the courts and functions also as quickly as they do. The same man is often indicted by the grand jury, found guilty by the petty jury, and condemned by the judge in the course of an hour.

The "Prosecutor for the Crown" told us: a multitude of criminal cases in the south of Ireland have their origin in the desire to possess land. In that part of Ireland there is no manufacturing, no industry, the people have only the land to live off, and, as they are accustomed at all times to live on the least that a man can subsist on, when a man has no land he really faces death. That is why implacable hatred and numberless acts of violence are born of *evictions*.

Part Three

Kilkenny, 24-26 July, 1835

20

Religion

Dr. Kinselly bishop of Kilkenny[24]
24 July 1835

Religion

We went to see today (24 July 1835) Msgr. Kinsely, bishop of Kilkenny. We found him very simply lodged. He told us:

My revenue is not large and still less fixed. I have only what comes to me by the voluntary gifts of the faithful, but I can sometimes give a dinner. I have a gig and a horse. I find myself rich enough and I would despair if the state wished to pay me. Last spring I went to London for the sole purpose of preventing such a measure from being proposed. It would break the union that now exists between the clergy and the people. Now the people regard us as their own work and are attached to us because of what they give us. If we received money from the state they would regard us as public officials, and when we should advise them to respect law and order, they would say, they are paid for that.

Msgr. Kinsley added: In 1828 I was in France. On arriving at Rouen I saw two sentries at the gate of the archbishop. What is that? I asked a French ecclesiastic who was accompanying me. It is a guard of honor for the archbishop. I do not like such guards of honor, I explained, they make [people] regard your archbishop as a representative of the king, much

24. Tocqueville's spelling of names and places was often phonetic. Those spellings have been allowed to stand in the text. Tocqueville is here referring to William Kinsella, the bishop of Ossory.

more than that of Jesus Christ. I afterwards saw the Corpus Christi procession. They marched between two lines of soldiers. What is that? I asked again. What are the soldiers for? Who wants a military display as part of a religious feast? I was at the seminary and said to the priests who came to see me that it appeared to me they were taking the wrong means to make religion flourish. They told me, smiling, that I was a revolutionary. I replied, I live in a country which is very much like yours. The mass of the people believe, but a part of the upper classes profess a different religion from ours or does not profess any religion at all. Far from trying to offend the people, we identify as much as possible with their interests and ideas. We attempt to show to our adversaries the substance of religion without laying ourselves open to their prejudices by emphasizing external details. We avoid contact with the state. We act as missionaries in a nonchristian country. If since the revolution you had acted as we have, religion would be flourishing in France. Avoid contact with the state. Never use force. A man is not married in the church, you go and tell him that his children are bastards. It is not by wounding men's sensibilities that one brings them back into the church.

Msgr. Kinsely went on to say: When I arrived at Paris I met an Irishman who had been my student at the seminary. I had refused to let him enter orders, because I knew he was completely incompetent: he had come to France and had been admitted to the priesthood. I told the fact to a vicar general of the archbishop of Paris, who told me: What do you wish? We lack subjects. I replied: It would be a hundred times better to leave a parish without a priest than to give it a bad one. I attended classes in some of your seminaries and I observed the students were very imperfectly taught and roughly brought up. It is not such a clergy that can raise religion. However, religion in France seems to me still to have deep roots. It still has a hold on the people.

I said to Msgr. Kinsely that it also had great friends in the highest classes.

I do not know, he replied, whether such friends are not more dangerous than useful to it. I remember having been taken by a priest in Paris to the house of the Marquis _____ whose chaplain he was. The Marquis X was a peer of France and his son a deputy. I spoke of the charter, and he told me that the charter served only to make rebels, and that freedom of the press was a curse . . . all opinions and maxims that could not fail to render him odious to the population, and that were directly opposed to the spirit of the times in which we live. They told me that many other persons in his position thought as he did. If it is so, the intimate connection between the clergy and the upper classes cannot fail to be opposed to religion, for, above all, the clergy must not be separated from the masses. A religion is not a government, it cannot be imposed.

21

Political conditions

Conversation with Dr. Kinseley.
(24 July 1835)

Conversation with Msgr. Kinseley bishop of Kilkenny
(24 July 1835)

Msgr. Kinseley is a very likeable man, very spiritual, perspicacious, and having enough sense to be impartial (as far as an

Irishman can be) and finding pleasure in showing it. There prevails in his language a certain note of triumph, which indicates the head of a party who arrives in power after having been oppressed for a long time. I believe that he is very sincere in wishing that the church should not be part of the state, but I wonder if he does not think, at bottom, that the state would do well enough as part of the church. These are nuances. I am perhaps mistaken.

———————

Q. I have often heard it said in England and even in Ireland that the Catholic population was half savage? The charge is probably false.

A. I am obliged to say it is true in part. But whose fault is it, if not those who have reduced them to this state by their bad government? What became of the Greeks under the Turks? Before 1792 we were not able to have schools, we were not able to be called to the bar, the magistracy was closed to us. We were not able to possess land . . . Examine the laws of that period [and] you will be frightened. Now, I confess that the population has some of the characteristics and unhappily the defects of savage peoples. These people have all the divine virtues. They have the faith. No one is a better Christian than the Irishman. Their morals are pure. Their crimes are very rarely premeditated. But they lack essentially the civil virtues. They are without foresight, without prudence. Their courage is instinctive. They throw themselves at an obstacle with extraordinary violence and if they are not successful at the first attempt, they tire of it. They are changeable, love excitement, combat. The Englishman, on the contrary, coldly calculates the odds, approaches danger slowly, and withdraws only after having succeeded. I visited an English general who had long commanded an Irish brigade. He told me: I could accustom my troops to anything, except to make them masters of themselves.

Q. Is the memory of the confiscations still alive?

A. Yes, as a vague instinct of hatred against the conquerors. There are still in a great many places families who are known to have been dispossessed. The family of Mr. Fitz[gerald], whom you visited in Carlow, possessed the great estates that you passed this morning, and which are now in the hands of Mr. X. There is in the county a family of laborers who [once] owned the immense estates of the Ormond family. But the direct line has been lost and no one dreams any longer of claiming their rights.

Q. What is, in your opinion, the principle cause of the poverty of the country?

A. A too-numerous population. It is certain that the land divided up, or rather not divided up, as it is in Ireland, cannot furnish a constant employment for our population. I believe that the consequences of absenteeism are exaggerated. It does harm but I regard it above all as a troublesome sign of the separation that exists between the different classes.

Q. Do you think that a poor law is necessary?

A. Yes, I believe so without hesitation. It would have, among other things, this result. Today, not only is there a shortage of land, but many estates have been converted into grasslands; those where 150 laborers would be found, ten shepherds suffice. If there were a tax on estates, the owners of these grasslands would find that they gained little by disposing of the land in this way; for if the land thus yielded more, and the landlord were obliged by the poor law to give all or part of his surplus in order to feed those whom he prevents from subsisting, he would restore his grasslands to wheat, or at the very least, he would no longer put the wheat to grassland.

Q. It is said that there are in Ireland now huge amounts of uncultivated land, which could be cultivated?

A. Yes. But up to the present, the farmer has been little disposed to invest in clearing land. Hardly was the land cultivated than the tithe collector and the state tax collector would appear.

Q. You have told me that morals were pure?

A. Extremely pure. Twenty years in the confessional have made me aware that the misconduct of girls is very rare, and that of married women almost unknown. Public opinion, one might almost say, goes too far in this direction. A woman *suspected* is lost for life. I am sure that there are not twenty illegitimate children a year in the whole Catholic population of Kilkenny, which amounts to 26,000 souls. Suicide is unknown. It is nearly unknown in the towns and still less in the country that a Catholic fails to make his Easter communion.

I say again that they have the divine virtues, but they are ignorant, violent, intemperate, and incapable as savages of resisting the first impulse.

Q. Do upper-class Catholics exhibit the same beliefs as the people?

A. Yes. Real unbelief is found only among some Protestants.

Q. Is it true that the Protestant aristocracy is very much in debt?

A. Yes. Nothing is more true. Most of them sink under their burden. Everyday we see the rich Catholics of the towns lend money to Protestants, and these latter end by being obliged to break *entail* and sell their lands. In this way many of the estates pass gradually into the hands of Catholics. We have seen lately in this county two Catholics, Messrs. X and Y, buy two estates, one for 20,000, the other for 30,000, pounds sterling.

Q. If the Catholics have a certain number of rich men in their ranks, why do they not send more distinguished people to Parliament?

A. The Catholic aristocracy has only been born. Furthermore, it must be admitted that the unstable spirit of our people shows itself in the electors as elsewhere. They nominated the most capable ones at first; then, they often replaced them badly. Perhaps Mr. O'Connell, because of his great talents, is an obstacle. He represents in his person the party.

Q. Is it true that there are village and family hatreds that often lead to acts of violence?

A. There were infinitely more formerly than at present. But they still occur very frequently. The government has long viewed these dissensions without sorrow. It feared [more] our unity against it.

Q. Was the government more tyrannical under the Irish Parliament than since the Union?

A. Infinitely more. All the penal laws are of that period.

Q. Is it true that in the past the peasants liked their landlords?

A. No. The peasants have never liked their landlords, and very few of the latter deserved to be liked. But they submitted with a patience they no longer have.

Q. But is the hatred not much more venomous than it was in the past?

A. Yes, I admit it. Because the fight is now begun and both sides seek to injure each other. Many of the great landlords no longer give leases, so as to prevent their tenant farmers from becoming electors; others give their farms only to Protestants.

Q. When did the agitation begin that led to emancipation?

A. For thirty years after the franchise was granted to Catho-

lics, they always claimed the right to send members to Parliament. This opinion became more and more threatening. In
1825 Mr. O'Connell finally decided to unseat a Protestant
enemy of the Catholics, in order to put another Protestant in
his place. This was a trial of strength. The county of Waterford
and the Beresford family, who owned nearly the whole county
and had represented it in Parliament for two centuries, were
chosen. Even the servants of the Beresfords voted against them.
The election was carried by assault. The following year, we
attempted the same thing in Kilkenny against a member of the
Ormonde family. We succeeded. Finally O'Connell decided to
run for County Clare. You know the result.

Q. What is the proportion of Catholics to Protestants in
Ireland?

A. In the South, we are 20 to one, in the North only 3 to
one

Q. Have these facts been known for a long time?

A. No. The Protestants maintained that the number of Protestants was much more considerable in Ireland than others
thought and they were opposed to a census. But the present
government has had it done. (Here the bishop showed us the
tables of the census for his diocese. In general they show the
most striking contrasts. In a parish where there are five or
six thousand Catholics and only 40 Protestants, there was a
church, two parsons, and the value of the tithes amounted to
nearly sixty thousand francs a year.)[25]

Q. But in proportion to the Catholic population, knowing
its rights and making use of them, one must begin to *reckon*
with it?

A. Yes. Undoubtedly. Care is taken in the South not to

25. The exchange rate in 1835 was about twenty-five French francs to one
English pound.

offend Catholics. Most of the members of the Protestant aristocracy of my diocese visited me on my arrival. It is not that
these gentlemen had ever heard of me, but they conveyed a
mark of respect to the representative of the Catholics, "(the
head)" of the county. Lord X, who is entertaining the lord
lieutenant next Tuesday when he passes here, took care to
ask me insistently to attend this meal. Often we correspond
unofficially with agents of the government or the administration who take our advice.

Q. How many Catholic priests do you estimate are in
Ireland?

A. About 3,000.[26] I count in this number only the parochial
clergy, the parish priests or curates.

Q. Have you priests for all your parishes?

A. We were short of them for a long time. But now we have
enough to choose.

Q. What is the revenue of your bishopric?

[A] 500 pounds sterling. But I am obliged to minister to a
parish, which takes up a large part of my time.

22

Grand jury

The grand jury in Ireland forms a kind of representative
body for the county; it is chosen by the sheriff. But the
sheriff is obliged to take at least two jurors from each
barony, which results in a little more complete representation
of the county.

The sessions of the grand jury are public, a recent act

26. The number of priests in Ireland in 1835 was something over 2000.

which already makes the measures of the grand jury more liberal and greatly diminishes the number of "*jobs*." The grand jury takes a much greater part in administration in Ireland than in England.

Information from the bishop of Kilkenny. 24 July 1835

23

Kilkenny Assizes.[27]

Criminal procedure.
Manners

Session of the jury at Kilkenny
25 July 1835

A light on manners
Criminal procedure

The first case threw much light on several details of criminal investigation and on the state of the country.

A man was accused of having been part of a gang that raided houses to steal arms by means of which they could afterwards exercise those acts of popular resistance that are called "*White-boyism.*"

The Crown had granted to the accomplice of the accused a full pardon on the condition that he would tell all that he knew and that he would agree to leave England [*sic*] forever.

We pointed out to the lawyers that such a procedure is faulty

27. See *Kilkenny Journal*, July 29, 1835, for an account of the Kilkenny Assizes.

on several accounts. Firstly, because it saves a guilty man, more infamous still than he whom it condemned. Secondly, because it serves as a premium for the most dangerous kind of false testimony, that which tends to condemn an innocent man.

They answered that it was an old custom, that the accused did not suffer as we thought because it is the rule to believe the accomplice only when other witnesses support him. The judge, in his summing up, recalls in effect this principle to the jurors. I persist nevertheless in my first opinion, the moral impression on the jury being the greatest danger the prisoner has to run and that impression cannot be subjected to the rules of jurisprudence.

In that same case, a "police-man" (gendarme) gave evidence of the admission that the accused had made to him.

This is even more dangerous for the prisoner than our system of examination.

The accused is condemned to deportation for life by virtue of the "*Whiteboy* acts."

The judge in his summing up pointed out to the jurors the frequency of these crimes, which consist in stealing arms without any motive of greed, but solely to disturb the country.

The second case was also characteristic of the state of Ireland. A farmer dismisses his servant. The latter presents himself at his house the following night, a Bible in one hand and a pistol in the other and forces him to swear an oath that he will take him back into his service. If an individual has taken a similar oath and fails to keep it, the one who made him swear it believes himself authorized to kill him.

These crimes are very common. There is nothing that better shows the imperfect state of civilization in Ireland. What a singular mixture of religion and wickedness. Of respect for the sanctity of an oath, which forms the foundation of every society, and of contempt for all the laws of society!

In order to prove the alibi of the accused, three witnesses presented themselves. The general opinion is that they affirmed a false thing. But a false oath, to save a man and to cheat a justice that oppresses and that you detest, is hardly culpable in the eyes of the people.

The third case was equally characteristic of Ireland. A farmer had been evicted from his land. The wife of his successor had been very badly treated in revenge. Nearly all the crimes of Ireland arise from quarrels about the possession of land.

While the jury deliberated in this case, the judge formed another jury before which he began the next case, without any loss of time. This was interrupted for a moment in order to hear the verdict and pass sentence.

General observation: In all the cases that we have seen, the jury played its part infinitely more quickly than a French jury, although unanimity was necessary.

24

Officials analogous to the public prosecutor

There is for each assize circuit an official called "*The Clerk of the Crown.*" There are six such officials in Ireland. They usually reside in Dublin. But they correspond with the magistrates and police of their district. It is they who prepare criminal cases and name the witnesses to be called. This is a limited public prosecutor, but nevertheless very useful.

Information gathered at Kilkenny. 25 July 1835

25

Political state of the country
Conversation with Mr. Pointdergast.[28]

Conversation with Mr.
25 July 1835 *Kilk*

Mr. P. is a Dublin lawyer. He appea
full of fanaticism against Catholics, which makes wha... ...
particularly interesting.

Q. It seems that crime has a tendency to diminish in Ireland?

A. For eight or ten months, it is so; but I do not see any permanent reason for such a thing.

Q. When did this popular justice called "White-boyism" begin?

A. About 1760. It began as a form of resistance to the tithe. Afterwards "Whiteboyism" extended to include relations between tenant farmers and their masters. When a tenant is evicted from his land, it very often happens that the crops, the livestock, of his successor, or more often still, the landlord's agent, suffers for it. The crime is never committed by the interested party, but by a man foreign to the locality and who has never seen the victim he strikes.

Q. Do you not think if this country separated from England, you would immediately have a violent revolution?

28. This should undoubtedly be Prendergast, and Tocqueville is probably referring to John Patrick Prendergast (1808–1893), historian, B.A. Trinity College, Dublin, 1825; called to the Irish bar, 1830; he published in 1863 "The History of the Cromwellian Settlement in Ireland."

A. I do not doubt it. I believe even that we will have one whatever happens. The time has passed when the evils of Ireland could be cured by gentle remedies.

We came to this country as conquerors, *we* English Protestants. The aristocracy of this country has always regarded the Catholic population as a bunch of savages; they have treated them as such. The latter are accustomed to consider the upper classes as their natural enemy. Now they have become strong in numbers and through political rights. The time for concessions on the part of the aristocracy is over. No one takes it into account any more and its kindness now would be turned against it. On the other hand, how is the country to be governed without it, for the Catholic population has really become savage. It is without reason. Its only aristocracy is the clergy. For the Irish, religion has become not only a matter of faith, but a matter of patriotism. All Ireland is under the influence of Catholicism. We now know enough about what the tyranny of the priests would be. We have seen only too well of late, at the meeting at Exeter Hall,[29] how abominable their principles are to wish ever to put the government in their hands. Ireland cannot then be governed, or govern itself.

Q. Do you think that the temporary dictatorship of England would not be a blessing?

A. Yes. But no one would consent to submit to it in Ireland. They regard the English as foreigners.

Q. What are the most common crimes?

A. Acts of violence that arise out of drunkenness, or village quarrels. Acts of premeditated violence that are committed to

29. In 1824 a group of Protestant Evangelicals had launched an association to provide a central hall where the various Evangelical societies could hold their anniversaries and meetings. After some seven years, in 1831, Exeter Hall in the Strand in London was opened for that purpose.

resist authority or to contend against the aristocracy. Theft is rare. You cannot imagine the hatred that exists between the landlords and the people. The landlords fear and distrust the people without concealing it. The people detest the landlords and very little would be necessary to raise them in rebellion against them.

Q. Do you not think the best way to loosen the ties that unite the people to the clergy would be to give the latter a salary from the state?

A. I do not think so. The Catholic clergy in every country and particularly in Ireland is to a high degree a domineering body. It has conceived the hope of chasing out the Protestants and finally ruling without hindrance over Irish society. They will not lose sight of that object; whatever is done, they will not now sacrifice it to an interest in money, and they will rather employ the money they will receive to facilitate that object.

Q. Do you know Bishop Kinsely?

A. No. We Protestants know very little of these gentlemen. At this particular moment, there exists between the members of the two religions a distance that you cannot conceive. Believe me, I have only *once* in my life dined at the house of a Catholic and that was quite by accident. We hardly ever meet them in society. Among the barristers here present there are about as many Catholics as Protestants. They see each other, but do not associate with one another.

Q. But is there not a natural tendency for a Catholic who becomes rich to mix with the aristocracy?

A. They would often like to, but they cannot. I am sorry to say that they close their ranks against them. The Protestants cannot accustom themselves to seeing them on the same level. They distrust them.

Q. But do you not fear that these men whom you reject will do as the middle classes in France, who became finally leaders of the people and led them on to a revolution that ended in the complete ruin of the aristocracy?

A. I believe that that will happen. But what do you wish? Matters have arrived at a point that the passions and not reason prevail. Left to their instincts, the rich Catholics are more aristocratic than ourselves. They have more distrust of the people in general than we do; we Protestants distrust the Irish, but, on general principle, we have confidence in the intelligence of the masses.

Q. The administration is still in the hands of Protestants?

A. Yes. Almost all the grand juries are Protestant. The sheriffs are Protestant. There is not a single Catholic among the judges.

Q. Given the state of the country, having a government thus composed, how do you not expect all the Catholics to become a nation apart?

––––––––––––

26

Violent and exceptional measures still in force

––––––––––––

The county of Kilkenny is still at this moment (25 July 1835) under exceptional measures of extreme rigor.

At a certain hour in the evening all the inhabitants must return home and the "policemen" have the right to enter the houses to see if this order is carried out.

The *Coercion Bill* was still much more severe before it was toned down a year ago, for then it permitted the government in certain cases to establish courts martial.

25 July 1835

The Irish population cannot possess arms. An Irishman requires the permission of a judge to bear arms. And if he does so without that, the penalty is a very large fine, and if he fails to pay it, imprisonment.

Numerous police force detested by the people.

27

Political state

---

26 July 1835, Conversation with Mr. George[30]

Kilkenny 26 July 1835

Conversation with Mr. George. Mr. G. is a young Dublin barrister. A well-brought-up and very likeable man.

Q. How do you interpret the *Coercion Bill*?

A. It is a law that authorizes the government to subject, in appropriate cases, Ireland or a part of the country to certain exceptional measures. Under the Coercion Bill the government has the right, for example, to oblige the inhabitants to be in their homes at a certain hour and to authorize the police to

---

30. This is probably John George (1804–1871), Irish judge, M.A. Trinity College, Dublin, 1826; barrister, King's Inns, 1826, and Gray's Inn, 1827; Queen's Counsel, 1844; M.P. for County Wexford 1852–57 and 1859–66; solicitor general 1859; privy councillor of Ireland; and judge of Queen's Bench, 1866.

enter the houses at night to make sure that everyone is there. It can have certain offenders tried by courts martial. . . .

Q. The Coercion Bill, has it been applied to several parts of the country recently?

A. The police regulations of which I spoke to you before are still applicable at this moment to the county of Kilkenny. Besides, you know that the Coercion Bill expires this year and that the ministers have declared that they would not ask that it be renewed.

Q. What was it that caused the Coercion Bill to be applied to the county Kilkenny?

A. In general the prevalence of the Whitefeet and in particular a terrible event that took place two leagues from here (Ballymack I believe) two years ago. It was a matter of selling the goods of a man who had refused to pay the tithe. As resistance was feared, 50 police marched to the place. But the population ambushed them from behind the walls of the village. 18 police and an officer fell on the spot, the others were put to flight. At this moment, the county is very quiet. It is about the same as Tipperary. I remember having seen at the winter assizes at Clonmel (county town of Tipperary) 200 accused, of which 50 were murder cases.

Q. I saw yesterday a man condemned at the assizes who had by violence sworn another to an oath. Is that a common crime?

A. It is one of the most common crimes in this country. You know that there existed for a long time in these counties gangs of which the object or the pretext was to resist the oppression of the aristocracy and to establish a sort of popular justice. These gangs call themselves "*Whiteboys*," "*Whitefeet*" . . . the elements always existed; but at this moment they are not in action. In general the manner of proceeding of these men is as follows: Some of them travel through the country at night armed. They enter the house of someone and force him to swear on the Bible that he will further their projects. If the latter breaks his oath, he does so at the risk of his life.* At other times they go to the house of a tenant who took the place of an unfortunate whom the landlord had evicted from his farm. The "Whitefeet" make him swear an oath that he will leave the farm. And if he fails to do it, he is killed.

Q. Do you see a remedy for the ills of this country?

A. I confess that I do not. The Catholic population has been oppressed for a long time; now it is no longer so, and I truly believe that at the time of emancipation the Protestants were quite willing to allow the Catholics to share all their political advantages. But the latter do not want to forget their old wrongs, they want not only equality, but domination. They want to put us in the position of a conquered people, in which we long held them. That is what we are not able to endure. A country has never found itself in a more terrible position. On the one side a small minority which possesses all the wealth and enlightenment in the country. On the other a vast preponderance of physical force. In England and in all the countries of the world, I think, the population is more or less divided into two great parties. Those who want to get and those who want to keep. Here it is found that those who want to get are of one religion and those who want to keep are of another. This makes for a violence between these two great parties unknown elsewhere.

Q. Do you not think that a temporary dictatorship exercised in a firm and enlightened manner, like that of Bonaparte after the 18 Brumaire, would be the only way of saving Ireland?

A. I think so. But England herself is unsteady. Her government is not secure. No party has a majority in England. How

---

*One sees that the oath was only a way in which these crude men sought to justify in their own eyes the murder that they wished to commit.

do you expect that it will take a firm political line? At the present moment, we believe the English government willingly allows us to be oppressed and places us entirely at the mercy of the Catholics. How could you expect it to be otherwise.? The life of the ministry depends entirely on the will of Mr. O'Connell and some sixty Irishmen who form his party.[31]

28

26 July 1835
Dinner with the bishop of Kilkenny

At this dinner there were two or three priests and eight or ten laymen. There were some Catholic landlords, some Catholic barristers from Dublin; among others, Mr. Lawless, a member of the Catholic Association.[32]

Dinner passed very quietly, but the moment when the servants left and the wine was on the table, the conversation turned to politics and took on a general and animated character. They spoke of the poor law, which everyone appeared to desire, except one single individual.

The circumstances in which this country finds itself, said the bishop raising his voice, renders such a law indispensable. Who supports the poor in Ireland today? It is the poor. The rich man looks at the poor over the top of the walls of his beautiful park, or if he meets him on the road, he responds to his entreaties: I make it a duty not to give anything to those

31. O'Connell's following in Parliament at this time consisted of thirty-two members. George, in mentioning "some sixty," is undoubtedly including those thirty-four who were elected as Liberals.

32. John Lawless (1773–1837), Irish agitator and journalist. Editor of the *Ulster Register*, 1817–19, and the *Irishman*, 1819–24; prominent in the Catholic Association (1824–29), where he frequently criticized O'Connell.

who do not work. And he does not provide them with work.
He has big and fat dogs and his fellow creatures die at his
door. Who feeds the poor? The poor. The unfortunate who
has 100 bushels of potatoes for himself and his family gives
annually 50 to men more unfortunate still who present themselves starving at the door of his cottage. Is it right that this
man wears ragged clothes, does not send his son to school,
and lays on himself the hardest privations to relieve the misery
to which the rich landlord remains insensible?

Go to Mayo. You will encounter thousands of men literally
nearly dead of hunger. The marquis of Sligo has, in the same
province, 70 thousand acres of land, the revenue of which he
consumes in England. And should not the law force this man
to give his fellows some part of his surplus? Why are so many
people dying of hunger in Mayo? Because the landlords find
it in their interest to increase their grasslands, and if they can
make a little more money, they laugh at us besides. At the
present time, gentlemen, it is the interest of the landlords of
Ireland to render the people as wretched as possible, for the
more the cultivator is threatened by starvation, the readier he
will be to submit to every condition they wish to impose on
him. Let us give the landlords an interest in making the poor
comfortable.

This long democratic tirade was listened to with enthusiasm
and interrupted several time by cries of "*Hear!*" from the
guests.

Where do we see, cried Mr. Lawless, a greater proof of what
my Lord has said than that which is happening in Dublin?
Who supports the poorhouse in Dublin? The shopkeepers and
the small tradesmen. Who remains indifferent to the destitution of the people? The rich. This state of things is intolerable.

The conversation followed its course in this way for two

hours. It was passionate, superficial, light, often interrupted by jokes and witticisms. I thought myself in France. Nothing resembled England.

29

How the aristocracy can form one of the best and one of the worst governments that exist in the world.

---

26 July 1835 (Kilkenny)

How the aristocracy can form one of the best and one of the worst governments that exist in the world.[33]

Imagine an aristocracy that was born on the very soil that it dominates or whose origin is lost in the obscurity of past centuries. Assume that, not being much different from the people, it can easily assimilate with them. Give this aristocracy an interest, in unity with the people, to resist a power greater than that of the aristocracy and than that of the people, but weaker than that of the aristocracy and people united together; so that the more the people are rich and enlightened, the more the aristocracy is assured of its existence; the more the rights of the aristocracy are respected, the more the people are certain of retaining the enjoyment of theirs. Fancy an aristocracy that has the same language, the same manners, the same religion as the people; that is at the head, but not above, the understanding of the people; that exceeds them in everything a little,

33. There is a marginal note by Beaumont in the original manuscript. It reads, in part, "this piece was written at Kilkenny during our stay there together (July 1835) with reference to a conversation in which we had established a parallel between the English aristocracy, and the Irish aristocracy, and after which we each had composed our *version*. Mine formed the beginning of chapter II of the first part of *L'Irlande sociale, politique et religieuse*."

[but] infinitely in none. Conceive of a middle class, rising gradually in importance in the midst of this *state of things,* succeeding by degrees to share the power and shortly after all the privileges of the ancient aristocracy, in such a way that money, which everybody can hope to obtain, gradually replaces birth, which depends on God alone, and thus inequality itself comes to favor the wealth of all, for each one then hopes to succeed in sharing the privileges of the few, a universal effort is made, an exertion of all minds towards the acquisition of well-being and wealth. Make of this nation a vast center of commerce so that the chances of attaining this wealth, with which one succeeds to all the rest, are infinitely multiplied and give at once to the poor a thousand hopes, and consequently a thousand reasons for remaining peaceable and satisfied with their lot.

Imagine all of these things,* and you will have a people among whom the upper classes will be more brilliant, more enlightened, more wise, the middle classes more wealthy, the poor more comfortable than elsewhere. Where the state will be as firm in its plans as if it were governed by one man, powerful and strong as if it rested on the free will of all its citizens. Where the people will submit to the law as if they made it themselves, and where order will reign as if it were only a question of carrying out the will of a despot.† Where each, finally being content with his destiny, will be proud of his country and will be determined on being proud of himself.

––––––––––

Imagine now an aristocracy that is established by conquest at a period so recent that the memories and the traces of the event are still present in every mind. Place the time of the

*It will be necessary to search for others. They are there certainly.
†Influence on the natural character.

conquest in a century when the conqueror had already acquired all the lights of civilization, and when the conquered was still in a state of half savagery, so that the stronger in moral power is also the more powerful in strength of mind, [the conqueror] placed in both respects as far as possible from the vanquished. Give to these men, already so unlike and unequal, a different religion, so that the nobility not only distrusts the people, but hates them, that the people not only hate the nobility, but damns them. Far from giving to this aristocracy so constituted a particular reason to unite with the people, give it a particular reason not to unite with the people, in order to remain similar to the nation from which it sprung and from which it still draws all its strength and to which it glories in being like. Instead of giving it a special motive of treating the people with consideration, give it a special motive to oppress them, by placing its confidence in this foreign support, which causes it to have nothing to fear from the consequences of its tyranny. Give to this aristocracy the exclusive power of governing and of enriching itself. Prevent the people from succeeding to its ranks, or, if you permit that, impose on that benefit conditions they cannot accept, in such a way that, left to themselves, estranged from the upper classes, butt of their enmity, without hope of power to ameliorate their lot, they end by abandoning themselves, and finding themselves satisfied when, after a thousand efforts, they can extract from their field what will permit them not to die,* while the nobleman, on his side, stripped of all that stimulates man to great and generous actions, slumbers in an unenlightened egoism.

You will certainly have a frightful state of society, a state in which the aristocracy will have all the faults and maxims of

---

*Seeks in violence a support that he cannot hope to find in the law.

oppressors, the people all the vices and weaknesses of slaves. Where the law will serve to destroy what it ought to protect; violence to protect what it seeks elsewhere to destroy. Where religion will seem to draw its strength only from the passions that it ought to combat, and exists only to prevent the hatreds from being forgotten and men from establishing among themselves the brotherhood that it preaches unceasingly to them.

The two societies I have just described were both, however, founded on the principle of aristocracy. The two aristocracies of which I have spoken have the same origin, the same manners, nearly the same laws. The one, however, has for centuries given the English one of the best governments that exists in the world, the other, to the Irish, one of the most detestable that could ever be imagined.

Aristocracy then can be subjected to particular circumstances that modify its nature and its effects, and it is very necessary in judging it that these circumstances are taken into account. The truth is that the aristocratic principle in England has been subjected to particularly happy circumstances, in Ireland to causes particularly disastrous. It would not be fair to judge theoretically aristocracy by either the one or the other of these two peoples. The rule lies elsewhere.*

---

*Here, to complete this piece, it will be necessary to inquire into what are the vices and the virtues most natural to aristocracy.

Part Four

Cork-Galway,
27 July-3 August, 1835

30

27 July 1835

Journey from Kilkenny to Kork

From Kilkenny to Mitchelstown the country has the same appearance as before. Hills despoiled of woods; cut up into a vast number of small fields. From time to time some great moors. Few villages, no belfries. One encounters churches without parishioners and one does not see those that have them. The habitations scattered along the road. The same kind of house, perhaps more wretched still than those in County Kilkenny. Houses of mud, roofs of thatch, often falling down. No chimney, or chimney so imperfect that nearly all the smoke comes out the door. No windows. A little dung hill near the door, a pig in the house. Some farmers in rags. Some children who relay on nearly the whole road and pursue the passers-by. I believe that these wretched dwellings contain beggars, but my traveling companions assure me that they are the dwellings of small farmers who have twenty or thirty acres to cultivate.

At Mitchelstown there is a magnificent mansion belonging to Lord Kingston. He owns around the mansion 75,000 acres. He lives there. I was shown a vast clearing that he has made and that is covered with fine crops and a row of clean and comfortable small houses that he had built for the tenant farmers. It is said that he has profited by these operations. The town of Mitchelstown has not, as much as the rest of the country, so wretched an appearance.

I ask where is the "Lord"? They tell me that two years ago he went mad. Why? I am told that it is because he saw himself charged with 400,000 pounds sterling of debts, without hope of ever being able to pay them. The money had been lent him by the Catholic merchants of Cork who hold mortgages on the vast estate that I had seen and who receive nearly all the income. It is the same in nearly all Ireland. See the finger of God! The Irish aristocracy wished to remain separated from the people and to remain English. It has striven to imitate the English aristocracy without having its spirit and its resources, and it dies where it has sinned. The Irish have been dispossessed by force of arms. They return to the estates by industry.

At a village I saw about thirty peasants seated in a circle at the door of a small house. They told me that this was the parish priest's house and that the men await their turn for confession.

We arrived at Fermoy, a rather pretty town on the banks of the river Black Water. The town seems comparatively prosperous. The source of this prosperity is the presence of two regiments of infantry whose immense barracks cover the neighboring height. A distressing source for a country's prosperity.

The entry into Cork is very fine. The merchants' quarter is handsome. In the suburbs are squalid dwellings and a population more horrible still, such as one can find only in Ireland. The Catholic bishop lives in a little house in the middle of this quarter. The shepherd in the midst of his flock.

————————

We had with us in our open coach two young men, each being very drunk. These young men aimed words at and made jokes to nearly all the passers-by. All, men and women, responded with laughter and other jokes. I thought I was in France.

31

Kork. 28 July 1835

————————

Difficulties of nearly all the Irish landlords, which prevent them from giving any help to the population, even when they would like to, [and] from improving anything for fear of risking capital, and squeezing the poor so as to increase their incomes, which makes the poor still more incapable of doing without them.

A new complication, particular to this unhappy country, and which must not be lost sight of, when speaking about it. One of the principle causes of the present state [of things] is there. But this cause itself is only the effect of a more general cause, which has made the Irish aristocracy a stranger in the country, and has led it to ruin itself by wishing to imitate the English aristocracy without having its manly spirit, and without knowing how, like it, to draw on the freedom and ease of the lower classes as new sources of wealth.

The duke of Bridgewater has doubled his fortune by opening a canal, the duke of Newcastle by opening coal mines. What would be the use of opening a canal in Ireland, where no one has "goods" to transport? Or mining coal that none can buy?

32

[Muckross Abbey. July 30, 1835][34]

The priest made his way towards a cluster of great trees which stood to the left at the foot of the hill. I followed him and soon I noticed through the trunks and above the tops of

34. From Tocqueville's description there is no doubt that this is Muckross Abbey. Muckross Abbey is said to have been founded by Donal McCarthy in 1440 for the Conventual Franciscans and dedicated to the Holy Trinity. In their *A Week at Killarney* (London, 1850), p. 137, however, Mr. and Mrs. S. C. Hall, the celebrated English travelers, note that the *Annals of the Four Masters* give the date of the founding of the abbey a century earlier, which would give greater credence to Tocqueville's reading of the date 1350 as the year in which John McCarthy, the abbot, died.

the tallest of them a gothic portal so covered with moss and ivy that from afar I took it for an immense tree surrounded with its thick branches. The rose window that had formerly decorated the height of the archway remained almost intact in the middle of the ruined monument. The priest did not allow me time to admire the remains of the ecclesiastical splendor of the middle ages; passing alongside the ruined walls of the monument, he arrived at a small pointed gothic door, crossed a dark corridor that took us to a square tower composed of flattened saxon arches and sustained by small gothic columns. It was the cloister. The earth and the debris were piled up in the narrow court around which circulated the galleries of this cloister. Bushes had grown there; their branches penetrated every part of the abandoned cloister and gave it an icy dampness.

We crossed these silent galleries and, passing again through a small pointed gothic door, we found the same church of which I had glimpsed the portal. The roof had collapsed centuries before, but the walls remained standing. The ivy had taken hold of the long pointed gothic windows; it had wound itself around the small columns and capitals. In the middle of the choir, an immense pine had taken root and had grown to the height of the building; there it had spread its branches wide and had enveloped the abandoned sanctuary in its shade. There reigned in this ruined church something of the damp unintelligibility that in the bosom of our great gothic cathedrals so well disposes the soul to a kind of religious terror. The church was full of tombs, but not all were dated from the same period. Near the wall, on the side where the altar had been, the remains of a marble monument could be seen on which I read these words written in gothic characters: hic jacet Johannus Mac Carthy hujus Monaterii abbas . . . The rest of the inscription was missing. At the bottom of the stone are found these words: Requiescat in pace Domini anno 1350. At the foot of this monument was a stone still quite white on which was written: Here rests Peter Mac Cudde priest of this parish. Pray for him 1820. All around were planted a great number of crosses of wood which did not bear an inscription, but only a name.

My guide sat a moment on the monument of the abbot. He cast a look full of melancholy on the walls covered with moss, and on these tombs that contained so many past generations, and he said: You see, Sir, one of the most beautiful monasteries built by the piety of our fathers; the Protestants have pulled down the cross, which surmounted the portal of this church, they have smashed the statues of the saints, opened the vaults and driven their flocks to gorge on the remains of the altar. But it is much easier to knock down stones than to root out from men their beliefs. In spite of the profanation of which this place has been the object, it remained a holy place in the eyes of the surrounding population. We have replaced the cross of stone by a cross of wood, and, not being able any longer to come to pray around this destroyed altar, we wanted at least our bones to rest beside those of our ancestors in the shade of this sanctuary.

There is something very touching, Sir, I said to the priest, in this fidelity. . . .

33

Memories of Persecutions

I found myself this morning (1 August 1835) on top of the coach beside an old Catholic.

He told me, while passing through Ennis, county town of County Clare: All of the country around here once belonged to the O'Connells. They raised a regiment for King James and, having been defeated with the rest at the Boyne, they were dispossessed. It is the heir of this family who, after two hundred years, has reopened the doors of Parliament to Catholics by standing as the representative for this same County Clare of which his fathers had once possessed the largest part.

This set my companion going. He went on from there to tell me what had been the fate of a great many families and a multitude of estates, passing from the time of Cromwell to that of William III with a terrifying exactitude and local memory. Whatever one does, the memories of the great persecutions is not forgotten. And when one sows injustice, he sooner or later reaps its fruits.

34

Catholic Clergy

Today (1 August 1835) I found myself on top of a coach beside a young Catholic who appeared to be very sincere.

I asked him for some information on the Catholic clergy and he told me the following.

A parish yields generally about 300 pounds sterling, but this sum is divided in general in three. The parish priest has about 120 pounds, the two curates the rest.

This salary is not much. Moreover it depends on the good will of the people; and after all it is not pleasant to live thus on charity. The result of all that is it is rare that the head of a wealthy family intends his son for the ecclesiastical state or that the latter chooses it himself. Such things happen, but it is the exception. The greatest number of priests therefore are the sons of large farmers. Those whom we call large farmers in this county are men who cultivate a farm of 125 acres. These men cannot be ranked as gentlemen and it is a real misfortune. Our clergy, however, are as a body very respectable.

I have quoted this conversation because it seems to me a rather good summary, which my experience of Ireland now makes me think is true.

35

1 August 1835 I dined today with all the barristers who follow the circuit. Half, I have been told, are Catholics, but I had beside me only Protestants and most of them seemed to me mad "Orangemen." There is one among others who told me that it was a mistake to blame the evils of Ireland on bad government. I then spoke to him of the times of the penal laws, believing that he would retreat. But not at all. He told me that at that time the penal laws were necessary, that they were indeed necessary to restrain by force men whom one could neither govern nor allow to govern themselves.

36

Mr. West.[35] Galway. 1 August 1835

Mr. West is a Dublin barrister. The Tory candidate of that town that O'Connell carried by only a few votes.

Q. Do you believe that a poor law will be useful to Ireland?

35. John Beatty West (1791–1841), barrister. Admitted to King's Inns, Dublin, 1815 and Queen's Counsel, 1840. In the general election of January 1835, O'Connell had received 243 votes more than West in a poll of more than 5000. West had petitioned against the results of the election, however, and O'Connell and his fellow Repealer were unseated in May 1836,

A. I agree with Mr. O'Connell on this point, that it would be harmful. In England, where there are 8 rich to one poor man, where the comfort and wealth are unbelievably great, in England even, they have difficulty in supporting the burden of the poor law. What would it be in Ireland?

Q. I have heard said at the three assizes that I attended that the number of crimes was decidedly lower this year than in the previous ones. What is the cause of this change?

A. It is due to the good will with which Mr. O'Connell and the Catholic clergy are favoring the present ministry. They keep the population quiet in the same way they stir it up at will.

Q. Is the power of Mr. O'Connell as great in this country as it is supposed?

A. It is immense, and unfortunately, Mr. O'Connell has a permanent interest in using his power to disturb the country. Mr. O'Connell, before becoming a politician, was a very distinguished and very busy barrister. He earned 5,000 pounds sterling a year. He gave up his profession to enter Parliament, and the Catholics since then have furnished him with a voluntary indemnity which often amounts to 10 or 12,000 pounds sterling. It is known that the sum is more or less great, according to whether the agitation is greater or less. You see therefore that his interest is creating a new cause of unrest as soon as the present cause weakens.

Q. Is it true that the Irish aristocracy is in debt?

A. Yes, "to a certain extent."

Q. What is its cause?

A. During the war, the value of land increased immensely. The rent on an acre (on the average) in Ireland is 1 pound. In that time it was 3 pounds. All the landlords had acquired certain habits and contracted certain obligations which they were

and the two Dublin city seats were awarded to West and his Conservative colleague.

not able to abandon. Such is the cause of their present distress.

Q. Do you not think the bill of Sir Robert Peel contributed to it?[36]

A. No. That is a great mistake.

Q. Is it true that there are a certain number of Catholic families that have recently become rich?

A. Yes. We had begun by refusing to Catholics the right of becoming landlords, then, in granting them this right, we excluded them from public functions, from which it resulted that all the intelligent men among them are naturally led to the acquisition of wealth, and, not having the same occasions to spend their money as the wealthy Protestants, they have rapidly acquired their fortunes. In spite of this, what most of the Catholics still lack, and what even in their interest prevents them from governing themselves, is the absence of an aristocracy. It is a huge body without a head. Unfortunately, one can say that in this country society is clearly divided into two parties, those who have the soil and the wealth, [and] those who possess neither the one nor the other. With few exceptions, all the landowners, all the landlords are conservatives. You can count on that.

Q. The new grand jury law, has it destroyed "jobbing"?

A. I believe that everyone agrees that it has increased it. (This is the first time that I heard such a thing.)

Q. Do you not think that it is a great drawback to have the grand jury chosen by the sheriff and to compose it exclusively of large landlords? Would it not be better to elect it?

A. I do not like elections applied to these sorts of things. They maintain society in a perpetual state of excitement and do not resolve either intrigue or *jobs* (*argument of a minority*).

Q. From when does the power of Mr. O'Connell date?

36. The reference is to the bill for Catholic Emancipation that was passed by Parliament in 1829.

A. He has worked for twenty years to acquire it. Mr. O'Connell is assuredly a man endowed with an extreme perseverance and an indefatigable ardor. But he has a profound contempt for the middle way, and among other things for the truth. His reputation began by meetings. There is no man who knows how to handle a crowd like Mr. O'Connell. He began by persuading the people they were very unhappy. He spoke to them of the injustices of which, he said, they (the people) were the object. He inflamed their passions and finally advised them to offer an illegal resistance to the collection of the tithe. In effect some individuals have begun to trample the law underfoot in this way, then others. The evil has become finally so general, most of the owners of the tithes have been constrained themselves to renounce the exercise of their rights.

Q. But where do you think he intends to stop?

A. When he is the absolute master of Ireland. I have heard him say himself that he imposed three conditions on the ministers to sustain them. To break the Orangeist party, to destroy the Church of Ireland (I forget the third).

Q. You have I believe a great number of corporations in Ireland?

A. Yes, a bill has been introduced in Parliament to ask for [their] reform, but we hope that the House of Lords will maintain at least the right of the existing "freemen" [to vote], who are Protestants and Conservatives. In Dublin, for example, where the chances are nearly equal between the two candidates, the two thousand "freemen" voted for me. You are aware that if the new law took away their electoral right, the balance would be turned. It would be the same in most of the towns of Ireland.

Q. Is it true that the Tories and the Radicals are face to face now in Ireland and that the party of the Middle or the Whigs is nearly destroyed?

A. Yes. The least advanced of the Whigs have become To-ries. The most advanced Radicals. Now, one can say Ireland is divided into two parties.

Q. I have often heard talk of frauds committed by the Catho-lics to become electors. What does this signify?

A. To become an elector, it suffices to swear that one pos-sesses the income required by the law. It is true that anyone can contradict the oath. But at the time of the Reform Bill, when the *"Registration"* took place the Orangeists were so depressed that they let matters go without looking into it. A multitude of electors swore a false oath. Others eluded the oath in this way. A farmer had 10 acres of land; but 9 were bog and virtually unproductive. He swore he possessed ten acres without making the deduction and he was an elector. In this way the majority of the electoral body is composed of false electors.

Q. But is not this evil repairable?

A. Hardly. The registration is good for 8 years and at the end of these 8 years, it will be enough for an elector to show his license to vote and he will be given a new one. This absurd law does not exist, as you know, in England. Once an Irish elector is registered he can be removed only following an inquiry by the House of Commons, an inquiry that can only give rise to great expense.

Q. Is it true that the Irish landlords squeeze their tenants as much as possible?

A. Yes. But they are very embarrassed themselves. Besides we have never acted as generously towards the tenants in Ireland as in England. Few farms in England are rented at their value. The practice in England is to divide the income of the land in three. One third for the expenses of farming, one third for the owner, one third for the farmer. A farmer who cannot find these conditions seeks his fortune elsewhere. Here it is not so. Furthermore our great landlords, by dividing the land excessively to increase the number of electors, have very much increased public wretchedness.

———

37

Conversation with Mr. _____ judge of the assizes court
at Galway[37]
1 August 1835

———

Mr. _____ is an old man much respected for his
experience and knowledge.

———

Q. Are acts of violence very numerous in this part of Ireland, quarrels between different villages, fights at fairs . . . ?

A. Yes.

Q. Does your experience lead you to think that these deadly practices are tending to increase or decrease?

A. I am convinced that they are decreasing.

Q. What is the usual cause of these quarrels?

A. The imperfect state of the civilization of the people, who take and like all the pleasures of coarse stimulation, such as the excitement of a fight and the display of physical force. The second cause, and the more important perhaps, is the love of strong drink. One drinks first and fights afterwards.

Q. Are the crimes committed in this part of Ireland of a very odious nature?

37. This was probably Charles Burton (1760–1847), an Englishman, admitted to Middle Temple, London, 1775; Lincoln's Inn, 1787; went to Ireland under patronage of John Philpot Curran; called to the Irish bar, 1792; King's Counsel, 1806; justice of King's Bench, 1820. When we consider that Burton was seventy-five years of age in 1835, was the father-in-law of John Beatty West (n. 35), and resided permanently in County Galway at Eyrecourt, it

A. In general, no. The murders are almost never premeditated. They result from a fight, not from an ambush. Theft is very rare; highway robberies are nearly unknown. There is no country in the world where the stranger has less to fear than in Ireland.

Q. I have seen on the different court *Calendars* many "*rapes.*" I have heard it said that morals are very pure. How can these two things be reconciled?

A. Morals are actually very pure. Nearly all the accusations of "*rape*" are made by girls who wish in this way to force a man to marry them. If the marriage takes place, the prosecution ceases, according to our laws. This behavior of the girls proves a great coarseness of manners but not impurity.

Q. Have you in this part as many "Whitefeet" as in the South?

A. No. There have always been many fewer. Acts of violence are rarely of a political nature.

Q. Are false oaths frequent?

A. Yes.

Q. Is the illegal imposition of an oath with the threat of revenge frequent?

A. Yes.

38

2 August 1835
A sermon at Galway

The Protestant congregation is in possession of the ancient Catholic cathedral; a handsome Gothic nave which is used by

seems quite likely that he was the Galway judge whose conversation Tocqueville reports.

the hundreth part of the population (the 99 others [who] are Catholics obtained permission only sixty years ago to build elsewhere at their own expense a chapel[)]. The church [the cathedral] is badly maintained. The paving stones are disjointed; one would say that they have difficulty in preventing the grass from growing there. The walls are dirty and have the appearance of being half-repaired. In the middle of the transept are a certain number of very clean and comfortable benches ("pews"). In the middle of the choir a large stove. All the rest of the church is deserted. The pews can seat two or three hundred persons. The presence of the court of assizes has almost filled them. All the rest are vacant. The entire congregation seems composed of the rich or at the very most of their servants [as well]. An hour before we had seen a vast population crowded on the bare paving stones of a Catholic church that was too small to receive them.

The preacher, who is a man who speaks well, attends to his delivery, has white gloves and a large notebook in his hand, goes into the pulpit. He utters some commonplaces about charity, then turning suddenly to politics, he explains that God indeed had prescribed the principle of alms-giving to the Jews. But he had never made it a *legal* obligation. That the principle of charity is sacred but that its performance, as that of all moral principles, ought to be subject to conscience, (allusion to the poor law against which the Orangemen contend in Ireland). Passing from there to the advantages of charity, he discovers that it forms the greatest bond in society and that he did not know there were any others. There are indeed, it is true, senseless and perverse men who believe that it is possible to make men equal and dispense in consequence with this bond that establishes the kindness and gratitude between the rich and the poor. But such doctrines are manifestly contrary to the will of God, who made men weak and strong, clever and stupid, capable and incapable. Society ought to form a consistent ladder and its happiness depend on the respect each will have for the rank of his neighbor and on the satisfaction with which he will fill his own. Opposite doctrines can be preached only by the enemies of order, by agitators who, after having deprived the people of celestial lights (the Bible), will push them towards actions destructive of civilization.

The preacher ended by assuring his audience that the collection was not intended to relieve the wretchedness of Catholics; without doubt all misery ought to concern Christians, but does not scripture say that it is necessary to relieve your own before thinking of strangers? And is not this moral especially applicable to a small body like that which the Protestants of Galway form, who need to be all united among themselves to endure as a living witness of the true religion, without the support of numbers?

I left thinking that charity, so restricted, will hardly destroy the congregation. For in Galway, almost all the Protestants are rich and all the poor, with very few exceptions, are Catholics.

39

Consequences of a bad government

Sometimes one learns important truths even from men most possessed by the spirit of party.

Mr. French,[38] barrister, Orangeman, told us today (2 August 1835) that people complain that the Irish are lazy and liars; but it must be considered that formerly they had not been able to

38. French has proved impossible to identify. In the list of admissions to King's Inns, Dublin, there are some twenty possible candidates between 1800 and 1830 who might be the French referred to.

acquire anything, which hardly gave any motive for industry. And they were obliged to hide and often to lie to carry out their religious duties. When the law operated in such a manner that lying could be bound to the idea of a moral duty, one must not be surprised that men lost general respect for the law.

Galway

40

Galway 2 August 1835

That when one allows the forms of liberty to subsist, sooner or later they will kill tyranny.

Nowhere is this general truth better brought into relief than in Ireland. The Protestants, in conquering Ireland, left the people electoral rights. But they possessed the land, and, masters of the fortunes of the electors, they controlled their votes at will. They left freedom of the press, but, masters of the government and all its props, they knew that it would not dare to write against them. They left the right of assembly, suspecting indeed that no one would dare to meet to speak against them. They left "habeas corpus" and the jury; being themselves the magistrates and in large part the jurors, they did not fear the guilty escaping them. Matters have been marvelously so for two centuries. The Protestants had in the eyes of the world the honor of liberal principles, and they enjoyed all the actual consequences of tyranny. They had a legal tyranny, which would be the worst of all, if it did not always leave the roads open to the future of liberty.

The time has finally come when the Catholics, having become more numerous and more wealthy, have begun to work their way on to the bench of magistrates and into the jury box.

When the electors are advised to vote against their landlords, when the freedom of the press has served to prove the despotism of the aristocracy, the right to assemble at a meeting has permitted them to become overheated at the sight of their slavery; since then tyranny has been vanquished by the very forms to the darkness in which she was always thought to live, and as whose instruments they have served for two hundred years.

41

Remains of the Protestant domination

In Cork they told us that all the officers of the corporation are Protestants (there are 80,000 Catholics in 107,000 souls). This corporation names the sheriff, who is Protestant, who names the grand jury in which there were only two Catholics at the time we passed through. Now the Catholics make up 4/5 of the population of the town, as I have said just now, and the 19/20 of that of the county. And the Protestants cry about oppression.

Galway 2 August 1835.

42

Galway Assizes[39]
3 August 1835

Trial of a Protestant minister accused of having seduced a girl.

39. See *The Irishman* (Galway), August 5, 1835, for a full account of this trial at the Galway Assizes.

I saw in Galway a very characteristic trial which throws a strong light on the social and political state of this country.

About sixty years ago a Catholic priest by the name of O'Rock became a Protestant and married.[40]

His son was brought up in the Anglican religion, became a minister, and thanks to the good example given by his father, was provided with the benefice of Mylock, a large parish in the neighborhood of Galway.[41]

Soon afterwards he was appointed justice of the peace and finally the court of *Chancery* charged him with the management of a considerable estate. The parish of Mylock is composed of 10,000 Catholics and about a hundred Protestants. The income of the rector was considerable, his duties few; as minister he demanded the tithe, as justice of the peace he saw to it that it was paid without resistance. To occupy his spare time, he bought or rented land and took over a farm (it is his lawyer who said this) of 1200 acres of land. All prospered for thirty years for Mr. O'Rock. He married three times, had a large family, established his daughters, placed his sons and lived in the hope of a happy old age.

Mr. O'Rock, by the fact of his birth, as may be believed, was particularly abhorred by Catholics, who formed the great mass of the surrounding population. He became far more [hated] still when the question of tithes was raised; he persisted in levying the tithe, while his neighbors agreed not to pursue it, and exacted it with the utmost rigor. As a magistrate he showed himself an inflexible and violent persecutor of the poor. He had, furthermore, the misfortune to attract the animosity of the local Protestants. Twice there were attempts to

40. Tocqueville once again has rendered the name phonetically. The correct spelling of the name of the defendant in this case was the Rev. John O'Rourke.

41. The parish of Moylough is situated on the Galway-Roscommon road some twenty miles from Galway (see map).

assassinate him. But he faced the storm and hoped to intimidate his enemies.

In the parish of Mylock lived a Catholic solicitor ("attorney"). The latter embraced with ardor the cause of his coreligionists, and with the assistance of legal means began the warfare against the Reverend Mr. O'Rock of which we have seen the last act.

This solicitor, who was called Killkelly,[42] set about watching the conduct of Mr. O'Rock. And every time the latter strayed from the letter of the law, Killikelly took him or had others take him to court. Seven cases thus succeeded each other in a short time. Mr. O'Rock lost them all and was condemned each time to pay his adversaries considerable damages and costs. Killikelly declared that his intention was not to apply any of this money to his own use. He bought a piece of ground opposite the house of Mr. O'Rock, and, with the help of the money extracted from the latter by the decrees of the courts, he began to build under his very eyes a pretty little Catholic chapel.

Mr. O'Rock, it appears, is known in the district for having irregular morals. Two years ago he had in his service the daughter of a Catholic peasant named Molly X.[43] Molly became pregnant. Her father chased her out of his house; her friends refused to receive her. But a shepherd of Kilikelly was more compassionate, he took her into his hut, kept her for six weeks. And the child having come into the world, Molly took it to the house of a local priest, to whom she declared that Mr. O'Rock had seduced her, that he had taken her honor actually inside the Protestant church of Mylock, and that he was the

42. Tocqueville has misspelled the name of the solicitor. He was D. Moore Killikelly, and Tocqueville has spelled it in four different ways, including correctly, in the manuscript.
43. Her name was actually Ellen Tanihan.

father of the child. The priest gave the little girl the name of Mary O'Rock and the news was spread through the county. Killikenny, having learned these facts, took the father of the young girl into his service, and he, at the instigation and with the help of his master (so Killikelly declared himself at the hearing), instituted the case of which we have been witnesses.

The jury is what is called a *"special jury"* (the parties agree on 40 names from which are drawn 12 jurors by lot). These jurors are respectable local landlords. The draw yielded 9 Catholics and three Protestants. But unanimity is necessary to reach a verdict. The room is packed. The two populations, the two religions are face to face. The case is followed with the most lively interest. Mr. Killikelly's counsel speaks. He is a Protestant; he knows, says he, that most of his audience have come with the hope of seeing the Church of England humiliated. But such is not his intention. He believes, himself, that the Church of England ought to expel unworthy members and O'Rock is of that number. In this way, he preserved his personal position and dealt only surer blows to the minister.

The witnesses are heard. Their animosity against the Protestant priest was manifestly apparent. However they are precise and unanimous. The audience is in suspense. The judge (a Protestant and a Tory) sums up in favor of the accused. The jury retires and after an hour, it returns and delivers a verdict of guilty. Everybody understands that such a verdict was a decree of banishment against the Rev. O'Rock and many people think that this motive has influenced the jury more than the proofs of the plaintiff. What is certain is that to us as strangers they did not appear sufficient.

The next day we left Galway to go to Tuam. Some coaches going in the opposite direction stop us. Well! What news? What did the jury decide in the case of Mr. O'Rock?—The verdict has been unfavorable to him—So, he is ruined?—and

this time at least, he will be forced to leave the country.—
What a blow for the Church of England! And we separate
with mutual satisfaction.

At the same assize two men were condemned to death and
executed immediately for having murdered and mutilated a
"police-man." It was thought the murderers had been moti-
vated only by the thought that he was a "policeman."

43

High cost of justice

(3 August 1835) In Galway a peasant pleaded that a minister
had dishonored his daughter and sued for damages [and] costs.

To prove that the peasant was only a straw man, the lawyer
pointed out that it would be absurd to suppose that a peasant
could afford the expense of such a case. And his opponent,
sinking under the weight of such reasoning was reduced to
admitting that the money had in effect been furnished to the
peasant by an enemy of the accused.

Part Five

Tuam-Mayo, 4-8 August, 1835

44

A Catholic priest and a Protestant Minister in Ireland

Begun at Cork 28 July 1835[44]

I had taken care on leaving Dublin to provide myself with a great number of letters of recommendation. I had them to men of all parties and principally to the priests of the two religions that divide Ireland. On arriving at Tuam in the province of Connaught I examined my letters and I observed that two of them were addressed to the same village. On examining the contents of the two letters I saw that one had for its object to recommend me to the Catholic priest of the parish, the other to the Protestant minister. I willingly seized this opportunity to see in a very narrow frame a picture of which I had already perceived the detached parts, and I set off. I left the coach at the nearest market town and made my way on foot to the village of X.*

At first I follow a beautiful short-cut which leads to a mansion, it turns to the right, I take the path to the left which opens into a valley. Soon I found myself at the entrance of a village which was built at the bottom of a valley, or rather a ravine, confined on each side by two rather high hills covered with pasture.

At the bottom of the ravine ran a stream which no doubt swelled in winter, but at the time this note refers to offered only an almost entirely dry rocky bed. Not a tree grew on its banks which offered this spectacle of nudity that goes with

---

*All this ought to be told very simply but better and with more details.

44. See "Note on the Text."

nearly all the water courses in Ireland. The bed of this stream, a little while ago full, just now dry, appeared to form the only road of the village of which the houses seemed to be flattened to find a place between it and the two neighboring hills. I quickened my pace to hurry through this unhappy village whose look repelled me. But in passing through I could not help observing what I had already seen so many times in Ireland. All the houses in line to my right and my left were made of sun-dried mud and built with walls the height of a man. The roofs of these dwellings were made of thatch so old that the grass that covered it merged with the pastures that decorated the neighboring hills. In more than one place I saw that the light timbers that sustained this fragile roofing had given way to the effects of time and gave to the whole of the place the appearance of a *molehill* on which the foot of a traveler had rested.* These dwellings in general did not have any windows or chimneys, the daylight entered by the door, the smoke exited by it. If one could see into the houses, it was rare that he saw any other thing than the bare walls, a rickety wooden stool, a small turf fire burning slowly and dimly between four flat stones. The stride of a stranger, whose footsteps only made the stones of the stream roll soon attracted the inhabitants of the village. I saw crowding to the door men, children, old people who looked at me with surprise.

The pig in the house, the dunghill, the bare heads and feet. Explain and paint that.

––––––––––

Further on I saw five or six men full of health and strength nonchalantly lying on the banks of the brook. If I had known less about Ireland, this idleness in the midst of so great poverty would have excited my indignation; but I knew already enough

*All this to be gallicized.

of this unhappy country to know that unemployment is the norm. One cannot earn his living by the sweat of his brow as God commanded.

I stopped finally to look about for an inhabitant whom I could ask the way to the priest's house. In this spot, the bed of the brook was narrow and one saw a thin stream of water deep and clear flowing fast between the stones which obstructed its passage. Near this sort of natural reservoir a small girl of 7 to 8 years was occupied in drawing water in an earthen jug. I went to her and while she was still leaning over the surface of the water, I said to her: Do you know, my child, where the village priest lives? At the sound of my voice the child quickly rose up and, pushing behind her head with her two little hands the blond hair which covered her forehead, she fixed on me her blue eyes full of shrewdness and intelligence. I repeated my question, the naiveté of which brought a smile to the lips of the child. "Come along with me, Sir," says she to me, her only response. And leaving her jug half full, she began to walk or rather to run in front of me, without seeming to feel on her bare feet the sharp stones, though heavy shoes did not save mine. Thus we reached a place in the village where the valley, coming to open out a little, permitted the village to spread out. We left the bed of the stream at this spot, and, after having crossed two or three miserable lanes, we found ourselves before a house whose exterior appearance announced at least a certain comfort. It was a little house built of stone, having four windows in the front and two stories. This house was covered with thatch as the others in the village, the rafters in good repair. All around the house stretched a little kitchen garden which a very thin hedge protected from the attention of the domestic animals. It was closed by a small gate, which one could open any time at will. The child who served as my guide opened the gate, crossed the garden, opened without hesitation the door of the presbytery. I then noticed very proper wooden stairs in the interior of the house that led to the upper floor. My guide climbed nimbly to the top of the stairs and, without taking the trouble to turn around to see if I were following her, knocked gently on the half-open door. A strong voice replied from within: "Come in." The door opened and we found ourselves in the presence of the man I came to see. The little girl on seeing him made a low curtsey and says, here is a gentleman who asked to speak to your honor. Good, my child, says the priest smiling, and my little guide disappeared in the twinkling of an eye. I gave my host the letter of recommendation that I had been charged to give him and while he read it, I examined with curiosity the man to whom I had addressed myself, and his dwelling. A square room, simple, but very clean and very will lighted. Some engravings representing religious subjects hung along the walls, a little ebony crucifix on the mantelpiece. On the table, a breviary and newspapers. By the side, a wooden chair against which leaned a thick knotted stick surmounted by a broad-brimmed black felt hat. Such was the scene presented by the interior of the apartment. The priest seemed to me a man in the prime of life; his muscular limbs and sunburnt skin testified to an active and healthy life. He was dressed and wore his hair like a layman.

After having glanced at the letter I had given him, he gave me his hand cordially and, fixing a firm and frank look on me, Welcome to you, Sir, says he, I do not know if you are Catholic or Protestant; but whether you are the one or the other you will have to fast today (it was a Saturday). I did not expect you, and you must be content with my dinner. As for sleeping, my curate left yesterday to visit his family in Galway and you may have his bed. I assured him I would be very comfortable in his house and, having led me to my new room, which was on the other side of the landing, he left me to give orders for dinner.

After a quarter of an hour, he returned to tell me that all was ready and we both descended to a room on the ground floor where the table was in fact set. The linen was white, the cutlery simple and the meal very modest. It consisted of a large piece of salmon, potatoes, and a kind of cake made in a hurry, the sole extra that my presence had occasioned. An old man, half sacristan, half valet, watched us with a tranquil and benign air and provided for our needs with great care.

The dinner, as one may believe, was short; and my host, noticing that I did not care for the English custom of remaining at the table drinking, said to me: I have some visits to make to several of my parishioners this evening, Sir, if you wish to accompany me; perhaps we will find along the road some opportunity to chat which we would not find here. I accepted the proposition eagerly, and my host having put his boots on and his stick under his arm, we went out together and entered the village. On seeing him the women curtseyed and devotedly crossed themselves, the men respectfully took off their hats. He saluted no one and did not seem even to notice the respect that he received. But walking on and without stopping, he spoke a word to each. How is your old father today, Mr. _____? said he to one. When will your wife be churched, John? said he to another. What name will you give your child? said he to a poor woman who was taking a breath of fresh air outside her hut. If your honor wished to choose it himself, said the woman, it would be a great joy to us. Let us leave this care to Providence, said the priest, smiling, let us give him the name of the saint whose feast day will fall on his birthday. Why haven't you sent your son to school these last few days? added he, in a serious and almost severe tone to a better dressed peasant than the others. Is it not up to you to set the example?

Going along like that we reached the end of the village where I had already seen those young people lying idly along the brook. I saw them from afar in the same place, but they got up at our approach. You were still then not able to find work today? the priest said to them. No, they replied. We went however to the farmer O'Croly as your honor advised us to do. But the farmer O'Croly himself has been evicted from his farm by the lord's agent. The priest hunched his shoulders as if he felt a heavy burden placed on them. What do you expect, my children, said he, the day will come perhaps when there will only be the lazy left to die of hunger. That time has not yet come. Let us have confidence in God.

We left the street of the village at that spot, and took on the left a little sunken road which led into another valley. When we had taken some steps along it, my companion stopped all of a sudden and struck the ground with his stick, and turning he said to me: Is such a state of things tolerable, Sir? God said that man would be obliged, after his fall, to earn his bread by the sweat of his brow; but here they go even further than the divine curse. For you have just seen men who ask only to work in order to live, and they cannot succeed in doing so, and when you think that, in Ireland, more than a million of our fellow creatures are reduced to this extremity, do you not say as I do that such a state of things cannot be tolerated much longer?

I have heard said, I replied, that the marquis of Sligo, who owns, I believe, large properties in this parish, has come to live in his mansion. Do you think that if he knew what was happening he would not seek to lessen the extreme distress that prevails at this moment on his property?

You must be very ill informed about the state of Ireland to ask me such a question, said the priest to me. Do you not know the aristocracy is the cause of all our miseries and that they do not alleviate any of the evils that they give rise to? Do you know, Sir, what prevents the poor man from dying of hunger in Ireland? It is the poor man.* In Ireland, Sir, it is the poor who provide for the needs of the poor, it is the poor who raise and maintain the schools where the children of the poor are brought up, it is the poor finally who furnish the poor with the means of obtaining the comforts of religion. A farmer who has only thirty acres and who gathers only a hundred bushels of potatoes, puts aside a fifth of his harvest to distribute annually to those unfortunates who are the most in need. The starving man presents himself without fear at the door of the thatched cottages; he is sure to receive something to appease his pressing hunger. But at the door of the mansions he will meet only liveried lackeys or dogs better fed than he, who drive him harshly away. In order to give alms the farmer will spare the manure for his field, he will wear rags, his wife will sleep on straw, and his children will not go to school. What does the lord do during all this time? He strolls in his vast estate surrounded by great walls. In the enclosure of his park everything breathes splendor, outside poverty groans, but he does not notice it. His doormen are careful to remove the poor man from his view, or if he meets him by chance he responds to his entreaties, I make it a duty not to encourage begging. He has big and fat dogs and his fellow creatures die at his door. Not only does he not relieve the needs of the poor in any way, but he profits from these needs by drawing enormous rents and goes to spend in France or in Italy the money thus acquired. If he returns for a short time among us, it is to evict from his estate a farmer who is behind in his rent and evict him from his dwelling, as happened to poor O'Croly. Does it seem fair to you, Sir, that this man with his 80,000 acres and

*Generalities on equality and liberty and its benefits. At the end of the conversation. Faith, piety of the people.

his 40,000 pounds sterling of income escapes all the duties of society, and does not relieve, either directly by providing gifts, or indirectly by providing work, the misery that he has caused, while the poor man deprives himself of a part of what is necessary to relieve the evils that are not his work. Our aristocracy, Sir, has a positive and continuing interest rendering the people miserable. For the more miserable the people are, the easier it is to impose the hard conditions in the renting of farms. Each day we see the great landlords, for an insignificant pecuniary advantage, change the system of farming and suddenly put out of work half the farmers in the district. I can still imagine, I said, that the great Protestant nobleman who lives in the midst of a hostile population is not very inclined to relieve public misery, but you have in Ireland a certain number of great Catholic landlords. Shouldn't they give the others example?

Not at all, replied the priest; Catholic and Protestant oppress the people in about the same way. From the moment when a Catholic becomes a large landlord, he conceives for the interests of the people this egotistical contempt, which seems natural to the aristocracy, and seizes avidly, like the others, every means to enrich himself at the expense of the poor.

Chatting like this* we shortly arrived at a house that, although larger than those of the village, had almost as miserable an appearance. What most distinguished it was a certain number of small windows, or rather holes of different shapes which had been cut in the earthen walls and in which the fragments of window panes had been placed. Some peasants were seated at the door, and inside I noticed the heads of several children. This is our school, the priest said to me, it is not at all magnifi-

---

*Church. Separation of Church and State. School. Education. Newspapers. Dying. Generalities in coming back again of equality and liberty.

cent as you see, but the desire the population has to learn makes up for the lack of means of instruction and the ability of the teacher. We entered the house, or rather the room, for the entire house formed only a room, contained about thirty children. The space was too narrow for one to be able to be seated there, and besides, the school did not have any seats. At one end stood the teacher. He was a man of middle age, barefooted, who taught scholars in rags. This school was in fact very wretched, but there reigned there, in fact, as the priest had told me, a fervor for work that is not always to be found in the wealthy English universities.*

We continued on our [way] and the priest took up the conversation again. Forty years ago, Sir, a Catholic who dared to give instruction to these poor children was severely punished. And they complain that the Catholic population is still half barbarous. You cannot imagine, Sir, the fervor of these unfortunates for learning since the means have been furnished them. The rising generation will not resemble that which we see. There lies the hope for the future.

But do you not think, reverend Sir, I said, that if civilization gains, the faith perhaps may lose by the change?

We would not know how to acknowledge such a consequence, Sir, replied the priest vigorously, religion rests on proofs too strong to fear the light. Besides, how do you expect, Sir, that these poor people should ever succeed in resisting the oppression that crushes them, if, on the side where wealth and strength are found, is also found knowledge? Education, Sir, is today a vital need for Ireland. The Protestants say the Catholic population is half barbarous, that it is ignorant and lazy. This is partly true, but whose is the fault, Sir, if not theirs who by a tyranny of three hundred years have reduced to this state the

*A sanctuary. Send some money.

most active and the most [intelligent] people in the world? These people will one day govern themselves; this moment is approaching, it cannot be far off; what would become of society if the poor, in becoming powerful, remain plunged in ignorance?

The English government, I said, begins itself to realize the danger. It is making every effort at this moment to create schools that are neither Catholic nor Protestant and where, as a consequence, Catholics and Protestants both can attend. Do you approve of this new plan?

Yes, said the priest, but up to now our parish was too poor to meet the initial expenses that the school established by the state requires.

And do you not fear, I added, that education thus separated from religion might be more deadly than useful? No, Sir, said the priest. On leaving school, the children come into our hands, and it is for us to direct their religious education. The school teaches them the elements of human knowledge, the church teaches the catechism. To each its part. All means of instructing the people are good. Education is a vital need for Ireland.

I have forgotten to ask you, Sir, I said to my guide, with what object was that group of peasants gathered together at the door of the school?

I was going to tell you, replied the priest, to show you at what point our population began to be seized by the desire for learning. The men whom you saw are poor laborers, who come at the end of their day's work and they gather at the door of the school, so that the teacher, after he has finished his lessons, can read the newspaper aloud to them.

And who provides them with this newspaper, I said.

It is I who receive it, said the priest.

What! I responded, do you not see any inconveniences in such readings?

What inconveniences? replied the priest. Is not publicity a great element in public morality? Those who wish to do wrong, do they not take care to hide themselves, and the best way of holding each to his duty, is it not to show him that he can do it only in the daylight? Freedom of the press, Sir, is the first weapon that the oppressed have against the oppressor, the weak against the strong, the people against the government and the great. Freedom of the press has existed nominally in Ireland for more than a century, but it is only today that it has become a real power.

We had then come to the opening of a small beaten track which, after having twisted through the middle of a meadow, ended finally in a cluster of elms rising at the foot of the hill round which we had come.

The priest took out his watch and said: Time presses, the sun is setting. I cannot resist the desire, however, to take you to those trees that you see over there. Let us quicken our pace and we will soon regain the lost time. He walked ahead and I followed.

We thus came in a few moments to the place the priest had pointed out to me. Three large walnut trees, loaded with nuts, bent with age, shaded a small country cemetery. Fifty paces further on were the ruins of an ancient church of which the Gothic arches covered with ivy remained still standing and were surmounted by a wooden cross, all worm eaten.[45] Beside these venerable ruins rose a small, quite new Catholic chapel surmounted by a cross of stone. The priest stopped for an instant in this place, and leaning against the trunk of one of the walnut trees, he cast a melancholy glance on the ruins and a look of satisfaction on the small chapel, which seemed to be risen from the midst of these remains.

45. Tocqueville has written the word "description" in the margin next to this sentence.

The ruins you see, Sir, he told me, are the only remains of one of the most beautiful churches built by the piety of our fathers. The Protestants destroyed it, but it is much easier to knock down stones than it is to root out religion from the hearts of men. The heretics have devastated the sanctuary, they have allowed their flocks to graze among the remains of the altar, but they have not been able to prevent the veneration of the people being attached to these insensible stones. We have not been able to come to pray where our fathers prayed, but we have continued to bury our dead in a place that has been blessed of old and that holds their ashes. Since we have had freedom of conscience, we have not tried to rebuild this broken monument. We were too poor for that, but we have at least set up on top of these ruins a wooden cross.

The priest, on concluding the words, picked up his stick, which he had for a moment leaned against the tree, and made his way to the newly built church. The church was a small building, roughly built in stone and covered with a roof of slate, whose mode of construction could be studied from the inside, for the church had neither vault nor ceiling; the floor was of beaten earth; the altar was of wood; the walls had neither paint nor pictures; they remained in the state the mason had left them. The nave of this little church was cut in two by a wooden platform, supported at intervals on pillars; it was a way of accommodating a large number of persons without increasing the extent of the building and the costs of its construction. This church had a very small number of benches and no chairs. At the time we entered, five or six peasants, some were telling their beads and [others] were [sic] kneeling on the bare earth, seemed lost in a religious meditation so profound that the noise of our steps did not attract their attention.

The priest said a short prayer and left. When he came back

to the walnut trees, he stopped again and cast behind him a look full of joy and satisfaction. You will see in a quarter of an hour, Sir, he said to me, a man who still remembers the times when mass was celebrated in a ditch, while a part of the congregation served as sentinels for fear of being seized by the agents of justice. Ten years ago when I came to this parish, we still celebrated the divine office in a barn. God be praised that we are now able to gather in a place that is consecrated only to the celebration of our holy mysteries; and this church, Sir, he added with an air of triumph, this church was built with the aid of voluntary contributions.

This chapel, I said to my host, is built with the greatest simplicity. I have, however, difficulty in conceiving how your parishioners were able to meet the expenses of its construction.

The whole diocese came to our aide, replied the priest. We quested among our brethren; the fervor and the good will of the people did the rest.* But we are forgetting that time presses, exclaimed the priest, casting a look at the sun, which was descending rapidly to the horizon. We are talking and it is necessary to act.

Having said this, he made his way with great strides to the hill, which was behind the ruins of the abbey, and, instead of following the path he had taken before, he crossed the meadow, which covered the flank of the hill, and began to climb with such rapidity that I had difficulty in keeping up with him. In five minutes we reached the summit, and I noticed then at a little distance a poor hut, which was, as I soon discovered, the objective my host intended in his walk.

It was one of those miserable dwellings that cover almost the whole surface of Ireland, a house of mud, without windows. The fire was lit inside, and the smoke, escaping through

*Union of church and state. The ardor of the people.

all the holes of a half-destroyed roof, from afar gave the whole house the appearance of a lime kiln. The door was open, and as soon as they saw us a man, a woman and several children came out to meet us. Well, Mr. O'Sullivan, said the priest anxiously to the man, how is your father? He is growing weaker by the hour, replied the peasant, and if your honor does not save him, I do not doubt he will die this very night. The priest said nothing and hurried on. We arrived soon at the door of the cabin; nothing more desolate than the appearance of its interior. A bench of wood fixed against one of the walls, a worm-eaten chest, some agricultural implements, were the only objects that attracted attention. The fireplace was made of four flat stones between which a faint small turf fire, which threw off much more smoke than light into the room, burned slowly and dimly. In a corner was lying an old man who seemed to be at the very end of his life. In order to prevent him from suffering from the dampness of the ground they had placed under him a little straw and ragged clothes. On seeing us, the old man made an effort to raise himself on his bed. The priest entered alone and said: God save you, my old friend. Amen, the dying man responded in a faint voice.

The priest approached the bed, he knelt down and, leaning over the bed, he heard the confession of the dying man. All the rest of the family remained outside with me and knelt on the threshold. The sun was setting by then. Its last rays came through the open door into the cabin, throwing there an unaccustomed light and for the first time painting with brilliant colors the cloud of smoke that filled it. As he spoke, apparent at one and the same time were the physical pain and hope on the face of the old man, the care and the anxiety on the features of the priest. Have confidence in God, my dear son, said the priest on raising himself finally; when one has had as little happiness as you in this world, and has known as you have how to profit from its miseries, one has nothing to fear in the next. I shall return tomorrow morning, he added. And he left. O'Sullivan, he said to the peasant who examined his expression with dread, your father is very ill, but his greatest danger appears to me to be his extreme weakness. Send Jane this evening, he said, pointing to a young girl of eight or ten years who made a respectful curtsey on hearing her name, send Jane to the presbytery this evening, I will give her some fresh provisions, a little sugar and a small flask of wine, which the patient should be made to take a little at a time.

We resumed our way and descended the hill and he said to me: I have already seen many dying people and my experience makes me fear this unfortunate man has not more than 24 hours to live. I expected to spend with you, Sir, the time before mass tomorrow morning, but I hope you will excuse me. I want to make a second visit to this poor man.

After all, added the priest, shaking his head sadly, this man is not so much to be pitied. I know that he is in arrears with his small rent. Tomorrow, perhaps, he will be evicted from his home; and although it is a very miserable one, he holds to it, Sir, as the only place on earth that can offer him a sanctuary. His son has more strength than he to support the sorrow that menaces the family.

We took the same road that we had diverged from in coming up. It was a little beaten path that descended, like a long ribbon of sand, down to the bottom of the hill. We walked in silence. The priest seemed preoccupied by sad thoughts. We thus passed again near the small white church surrounded on all sides by the great ivy-covered ruins of the abbey and the simple tombstones of the village.

I stopped for a moment to consider again these objects and, renewing the conversation, I said to the priest, I see all the efforts made by this poor population to raise up its altars again, and I cannot help being indignant when I think that you are forced to rely on your own resources.

What must be deplored, replied the priest, is that the tyranny of the government, the exactions of the aristocracy, and the greed of the Protestant clergy have reduced this unfortunate people to such a degree of misery and unhappiness that it should be so difficult for them to provide, even in an imperfect way, for the expenses of their religious ceremonies.

What! I replied, do you not think that it is regrettable that the government does not take upon itself the building of churches and endowing the clergy? If that were so, would not religion be more honored, its ministers more respected and independent?

It is only the enemies of our Holy Religion, the priest replied forcefully, who hold such language; only those who wish to break the bonds that unite priest and people. You have seen, Sir, how I am looked upon in this village. The people love me, Sir, and they have reason to love me, for I myself love them. They have confidence in me, and I in them. Every man considers me in some way as one of his brothers, the eldest in the family. How does this happen, Sir? It is that the people and I every day have need of each other. The people share liberally with me the fruit of their labors, and I give them my time, my care, my whole soul. I am nothing without them, and without me they would succumb under the weight of their sorrows. Between us there is a ceaseless exchange of affectionate feelings. The day when I should receive money from the government the people would not look upon me as one of their own any longer. On my side, I should perhaps be tempted to believe that I no longer depended on them. Little by little we would become strangers to each other, and one day perhaps we should consider ourselves as enemies. Then, Sir, I should become useless to the very government that paid me. If I preach today peace and patience, I am believed because no one supposes that I have any interest in holding to such language, but if they could see in me an agent of the state, what weight would my opinion have?*

But do you not think, I said to the priest, that if you lost something on the side of the people, you would regain it on the side of the upper classes, to whom you would find yourself much closer?

We would lose by the change, said the priest, and religion also. It is in the people, Sir, that the root of beliefs is found. It is they who firmly believe in another world because they are unhappy in this one; it is they whose simple and naive imaginations lead them without reserve to faith. Any religion that will wander away from the people, Sir, will move away from its source and will lose its principal support. It is necessary to go with the people, Sir. There lies strength; and to remain united with the people, there is no sacrifice that one should regret imposing on oneself.

Inequality of the [distribution of the] land. Resistance to the law permitted. Discussion. Generalities about politics. Sovereignty of the people. Its capacity. Its understanding of its true interests. Praise of the Irish. We arrive at the presbytery. Do not say these things in France, you would be taken for a Protestant minister.

The next day, the priest [is] absent. I want to go to the Protestant minister's house. Answer of a woman whom I asked the way. Met the priest all drenched. I tell him where I am going. Tells me that he has never been down the hill, though he had often been on top. I climb. From the top, description of the mansion. Gothic style. Greenhouses. Grounds. Deer.

*No connection between church and state!

Wall all around. I do not see the church. At last I see it, standing out clearly, small gothic church, cut stone and open work. Handsome house at its side in the middle of a garden of flowers. The church is closed, but they are going to open it. Sunday. The minister returned a short time ago from a trip to Italy for his health. Inside the church. Stove. Carpet. "Pews." Two or three rich landlords. Many servants. Frail appearance of the priest. Sermon on moral obligations very well composed. Allusion to Saint Bartholomew, 29 August. On leaving the church I hand him my letter. I find an amiable man with very distinguished manners. He takes me to his house. He introduces me to his wife. To his daughter. Apologizes that she cannot play the piano because it is Sunday. Regrets the absence of his son, an officer who would have shown me the lord's park to which he always has access. Conversation turns on some subjects treated by the priest. Education must be directed in a certain way to be good. Press which can lead astray. "Kildare Place" Society.[46] Need for an aristocracy, for a national church, for a clergy richly endowed by the state. Incapacity of the people in general and above all the Irish people to govern themselves. Savages.

Do not say all this in France, you would be taken for a Catholic priest.

Could not offer me dinner because he dines with the "Lord."

———————

Return. At the top of the hill, on one side the hovels of the village and the little home of the priest.

46. "Kildare Place Society," or the Society for Promoting the Education of the Poor in Ireland, had been founded in December 1811 on the principle of providing non-sectarian education. The society received its first annual grant of £6000 from Parliament in 1816, and in its last year before the founding of the national system of education, it received £30,000 for the support of more than 1600 schools and nearly 138,000 pupils. After 1820 the society had fallen into disfavor with Catholics in general, and O'Connell in particular,

On the other the mansion, the grounds, and the smoke, which rises above the trees that surround the house of the minister.

Reflections. There wealth, knowledge, power; here strength. Difference in language according to position. Where to find the absolute truth.

45

New-port pratt 6 August 1835

In the newspapers we saw an article by a Mr. Hughes, parish priest of Newport pratt, revealing that the people of his parish were starving and asking for help.[47] We thought that we should go there to see Ireland in all its wretchedness. We left Castlebar at 10 in the morning and went to Newport pratt. The country between looked like almost all that we have seen in Ireland. Hills stripped of trees; valleys with peat bogs at their bottoms. Miserable huts scattered here and there. A severe and desolate appearance, even with a beautiful harvest on foot.

Newport is a village built on the banks of a little river that, a half league further, empties into the ocean. The glen is pretty. Two country houses surrounded by trees. In the village some clean two-storied houses. The parish has 11,000 inhabitants, 100 hamlets. It contains about 400 Protestants.

We are surprised at seeing the village street and the quay filled with a great crowd of men, women and children. Some are seated on the bare ground, the rest are in a group. Our arrival generates a great sensation. We are surprised. They

---

who began agitating for a Parliamentary grant for Catholic schools, and accused the Kildare Place Society of promoting proselytism.

47. James Hughes, P.P., Newport-Pratt. See Introduction, n. 22, for Hughes's letters to the press.

look at us with an avidity that we cannot understand. We leave our carriage and walk for some time in the street. More than a hundred persons follow us, without any demonstration but with a singular tenacity. Two or three speak to us; we understood that they took us to be government agents sent to relieve the distress. We ask where is the house of the parish priest. They showed us. Small white house covered with large white slates. One story. Three windows in front. A little stone peristyle. At the side of a little meadow. The priest is absent; some fifty individuals seated around his door appear to be waiting for him. We leave our cards and go for a walk. We come back after an hour. The priest sees us and asks us to come in. A man of about fifty. An open and energetic face. A little stout. Strong accent. A little common. Dressed in black with riding boots. He brings us in by a little vestibule, clean enough, into a small room on the ground floor, where two neighboring parish priests were already gathered. The walls are covered with colored engravings of Jesus, the Virgin Mary, the Pope and one or two religious scenes. Among all these pictures are tacked political caricatures. On the table are newspapers. The furniture is old but comfortable.* We tell the priest that we read his letters in the newspapers, that we could not believe the extent of the evils of which he speaks, and that we came expressly to assure ourselves of the reality. He seems pleased that such is our intention. He tells us that he will allow us to leave only when we should be assured that he told the truth and invites us to dinner. During this time the whole crowd that we had seen in the street, knowing of the priest's return, was gathered in front of his door. We ask him what the crowd meant; he replies: I succeeded by means of the

---

*Unmatched furniture. A walnut table covered with an old cloth. A small sofa covered with a _____ _____ material. Mahogany chairs with horsehair cushions.

publications you have seen in collecting about three hundred pounds sterling. I received just now 40 more, he added, drawing them out of his pocket with an air of triumph and extreme satisfaction; I have just organized a committee, three Catholics, three Protestants, to distribute this money under my supervision. We have bought oatmeal with this money; it arrived here two days ago, [and] I have put it in a shop that you see over there. The problem now is how we shall distribute it. All these people that you see, he said, pointing to the crowd, are here in the hope of participating in this distribution.

We. But are all these people truly in need of help.

The priest. Most of them have not eaten since yesterday. Since this morning they are waiting there fasting. These men are small farmers paying a rent. The potato harvest partially failed last year, the scarcity since last March has begun to make itself felt. Those who had cows, sheep, and pigs have sold them in order to live. All those you see there have nothing more. For we give help only to those who no longer can sell anything to help themselves. For several months these unfortunates whom you see have been constantly therefore on the point of starving. They never eat their fill. Most of them have been forced to dig up the new harvest and feed themselves on potatoes as large as nuts, which make them ill.

At this moment, the priest opened the window facing the crowd. All the spectators immediately fell into a profound silence. The cry *"hear hear"* passed from mouth to mouth, and the priest, placed as in a pulpit, spoke roughly in these terms partly in English, partly in Irish:

I want you to know that our flour has finally arrived, but several members of the committee think that it would be better to try to sell a part of it. Mark, that it is a question of a sale at half price. I also think that it would be desirable that it be done so. Consider it well, and if you have some resources, bring us your money. The flour will be sold at half price and with what we will get, we will buy more. It is therefore in your interest to make, if it is possible, the effort we are asking of you. You see that we will not let those starve who absolutely cannot do what I advise. I have some bad news to tell you; the absence of several members of the committee, and the lack of time to make a correct list of the most necessitous among you, will prevent us from making the distribution this evening. Arm yourselves with patience. Those of you who still have some provisions, I say to you in the name of God, share them this evening with your neighbors and friends. Tomorrow help will come. He who would let his neighbor die for the deed of not giving him a potato, he is a murderer. Disperse. Go home. May God bless you. I have one last recommendation to make, he added: Do not eat, if possible, half-ripe potatoes, as you have done these last days. We have had several sick for that reason. Nothing is more unhealthy than eating unripe food.

This speech was made in a loud and animated voice. One saw in his face when he spoke the passionate interest that he had for the people, but at the same time an air of firmness and command. There was more kindness than gentleness in his voice. The crowd listened to him in silence. All eyes were fixed on him. Mouths were hanging open. The pale cheeks and the tired appearance of these unfortunates showed their suffering. From time to time one of the spectators made an observation in a loud voice. The priest argued with him a moment and then took up his discourse again. When he had finished speaking, a part of the crowd returned in silence, with resignation and order. The rest sat down again at the door and seemed to hope that in spite of his words, the priest would not be able to refrain from giving some help that evening.

After dinner we wanted to go out. The door was still congested. From the top of his steps, the priest spoke again to his people. He said that he could not help them all, and that he did not wish to choose between them. Your misery, he added, will have an end because it will become known. Here are, he said, pointing to us, two strangers who have come to this country only to learn the extent of your sufferings and make them known in their country; God bless them, shouted the crowd. They are our brothers, said the priest, they are Catholics like us. I hope, he added, fixing his eyes on some Protestants who were in the crowd, that in this language there is nothing that wounds you. You know that when it is a question of charity, I make no difference between Catholic and Protestant. Jesus Christ shed his blood for all, and all are made in the image of God.

We passed through the crowd, which respectfully opened a path for us. In spite of all his efforts, the priest, who seemed very troubled, was not able to prevent himself from being concerned by the sight of some more wretched than others. I saw him slip a few small coins into some hands.

After the walk we returned. The priest showed us some very interesting statistical documents which I shall enumerate later. The conversation became general.

The priest. I have just shown you by my accounts, [and] you have judged, and above all you will judge tomorrow, the extent of our miseries. My colleagues will tell you that it is about the same in their parishes.—Yes, said the two priests. We have constantly before our eyes the spectacle that you have just seen. This state of society is intolerable and cannot last.

We. But all these parishes belong to a small number of landlords, the marquis of Sligo, Sir O'Donnel . . .[48] These men

48. The marquis of Sligo, who resided at Westport House, some eight miles from Newport-Pratt, owned more than 100,000 acres in County Mayo. Sir Richard Annesley O'Donnell (1808–67), who succeeded his brother as the fourth baronet in 1828 and resided at Newport House, owned some 7,500 acres in the neighborhood.

participate undoubtedly in works of charity during these times of distress.

The three priests, hotly and bitterly. It is an error, Sirs, these great landlords give nothing, do nothing, to prevent this unfortunate population from dying of hunger. It is the poor who support the poor.

We. But what is the cause of this?

The priest. There are several causes; almost all the great landlords are very embarrassed. Moreover, there is a profound hatred between them and the population. All the great families of this country are Catholics who have become Protestants to keep their property, or Protestants who have seized the property of Catholics. The population regards them as apostates or as conquerors and detests them. In return they do not feel any sympathy for them. They let the farmers die before their eyes or evict them from their miserable dwellings on the slightest pretext.

We. The resignation of these people seems very great?*

The priest. It is in fact. You have just seen two hundred unfortunates who are in real danger of starving to death and who can barely keep alive. Well, on the surrounding grasslands the marquis of Sligo has a thousand sheep; and several of his granaries are full. The population has no idea of seizing these

*Sheep. Harvests respected by the starving. Gentleness. Resignation of the population does not come from Christian virtue, but from abasement caused by tyranny, from the fear of the gibbet and transportation. Said in a way to make one believe that a little more impatience and energy would not be displeasing. Without religious duty, could not support such a tyranny. Education the only remedy for these evils. Efforts made for that. Quarrel with the Rector (850 pound income[)] House in view, pretty pavilion covered with blue slate rising up in the middle of tall trees with a charming view. Quarrel with the local aristocracy. Christian virtue of the population. Only one adult does not go to confession. Confession twice a year. A fixed time in each village. Fervor of the people for their religion. Financial efforts made for proselytizing useless. Priests who travel twenty miles into the mountains.

means of subsistence. They would sooner die than touch them.

We. That shows admirable virtue.

The priest. You must not have any illusions, Sirs. Religion doubtlessly counts for much in this patience; but fear counts for even more. This unfortunate population has been so long a butt for so cruel a tyranny, it has been so decimated by the gibbet and transportation, that all energy has finally left them. They submit themselves to death sooner than resist. There is not a population on the continent that in the face of such miseries would not have its *Three Days*.[49] And I confess that if I were in their position, and if I were not restrained by the strongest religious passions, I would indeed have difficulty in not revolting against this tyranny and unresponsive aristocracy.

These last words were spoken with a singular bitterness and were heartily echoed by the two other priests present. It was evident that these men, if they were not encouraging the people to revolt, would not be in the least sorry if they did revolt, and their indignation against the upper classes was lively and deep.

The priest added: The only effectual way to raise up again the demoralized spirits of these unfortunates is to educate them with open hands. Consequently, that is what we have undertaken, and we are doing it with all our might. You will see our schools tomorrow. The Protestants maintain we like the darkness. They will soon see that we do not fear the light.

The little house of the priest faced the quay. Three hundred paces from there, the river divided in two branches. The promontory that jutted out beween the two streams formed a hill,

49. The "*Three Days*" referred to by Hughes are an allusion to the July Revolution of 1830 in France when the Paris populace set up barricades between July 27 and 29, defying the army and police, and finally brought down the regime of the last of the Bourbons, Charles X (1824–30), replacing him with Louis Philippe (1830–48).

the center of which was occupied by a handsome meadow, the banks by tall trees. In the middle of the meadow stood a pretty square pavilion, covered with blue slates. We admired this residence on arriving.

To whom does this dwelling belong we asked the priest?

He replied: To the Protestant rector of this parish.

The conversation turned to this subject, and we learned that the priest and the minister were at open war, and they fought for souls with a very great fervor.* They attacked each other in the newspapers and in the pulpit in very bitter style. I saw some examples of the controversy. I recall that the Protestant minister called the Catholic "a blood thirsty priest." I do not recall what epithets the priest used, but they were hardly more complimentary. The priest did not conceal from us any longer that he was on chilly terms, at least, if not quarrelling with the large local landlords. He was himself the son of a large local farmer. All his passions, all his ideas, clearly tended to democracy.

We questioned him about the beliefs of the people. He told us:

The population has a living faith and an enthusiasm for religion. In this parish of more than 10,000 Catholics, I know only one adult who does not go to confession. General confession takes place twice a year. I announce from the pulpit that I shall make my round at such a time, fixing a day for each village. All the penitents must assemble that day at the place and the hour appointed and I hear their confessions one after the other.

---

*All the "police-men" Protestants. All the justices of the peace except one Protestants. Good reception of the priest in a Protestant home.

46

Why it is necessary sometimes to distinguish between good morals and modesty.

In Ireland, where there are hardly any illegitimate children, and where consequently morals are very pure, the women take less care to cover themselves than in any country in the world, and the men seem not to have any repugnance to showing themselves almost naked. I have seen young girls bathing naked in the sea a short distance from young men.

In England where one in 18 births, I believe, is illegitimate and where the morals of the lower classes are decidedly loose, modesty is carried to a kind of ridiculous affectation.

Does not what is called *modesty* therefore derive rather from the state of civilization than from that of morals? Or rather is not external modesty a combination of these two things? Does not extreme modesty derive from extreme civilization united with rather suppressed and well-regulated morals?

This worth going into *deeply*.

47

8 August 1835 Castlebar

I saw today the "chief constable" of Castlebar. He is the man who commands all the "police men" of the county. He tells me that he has 250 men under him scattered in the different parishes.

I ask him if crimes are frequent in the county; answers yes, but they are less frequent than in the South and of a less *insurrectional* nature. The "Whitefeet" system less known. He believes, moreover, that the number of crimes is gradually diminishing in Ireland. For twenty years he occupied a similar position in Clonmel. During that time the "Insurrection Act" was in force. Every man who was found away from his home after sunset without *a pass* was *transported*. In spite of that the number of crimes was frightening. The "police-men" were able to go out only in a group.

Asked if he believes that this country is threatened by civil war. Answers that the peasants are very ready for civil war, but the difficulty is to find leaders to lead them. Everybody who has some property equally dreads civil war because they know that once the torrent breaks its banks, all property runs an equal danger.

Unfortunately, he adds, in this country politics and religion are one. If it was [*sic*] politics only we should easily manage the population. Speak to the common man in Ireland. You will manage to make jokes about the poverty, about the oppression that is his lot. Say to him one word about his religion, he becomes sullen and turns his back on you. Take our goods but do not touch our beliefs. Such is the cry that reverberates a thousand times among the agricultural population of Ireland.

Our speaker, although an agent of the government, is evidently half an Orangeman, if he is not entirely one.

Postscript

Postscript

The Tocqueville that emerged from his Irish notes and letters was both an attractive and a complicated figure. He was at once a moralist, who was full of righteous indignation at man's inhumanity to man, and a social scientist, who was an astute connoisseur of the problems of political power. As a moralist, he was deeply disturbed by the Irish peasant's ambivalence towards the law, shocked by the appalling poverty of the people, understanding of their hatred for their feckless aristocracy, and touched by their simple and pious attachment to the faith of their fathers. He was also a compassionate, tolerant, and humane man, who had a nice, if slightly ironic, sense of humor. His humanity, moreover, was enhanced by a sincere love of liberty that was ever his morning and evening star. Indeed, the moralist dimension of Tocqueville was self-evident in his notes.

As a social scientist, of course, Tocqueville was also deeply interested in and concerned about these problems presented in Ireland by the law, poverty, aristocracy, and religion, but to the social scientist, as distinguished from the moralist, they posed difficulties to be solved rather than wrongs to be righted. Because so many of Tocqueville's notes were in the form of interviews and conversations, the questions he set, as an apparently detached and neutral observer, had a tendency to mask his own opinions. A careful reading of his notes, however, and especially a closer examination of his questions, reveals a great deal not only about Tocqueville's preconceptions and assumptions with regard to Ireland, but also about what he thought was required in 1835 to solve its problems.

If the Irish aristocracy, for example, was doomed as a class, as Tocqueville certainly believed it was, the real question for the future was who was to inherit the Irish political earth? If the Irish democracy, moreover, was that aristocracy's inevitable residuary legatee, what was to be done about the apparently all-powerful political influence of the Roman Catholic clergy with that democracy? Tocqueville was certainly aware of the dangers of a clerical political ascendancy in Ireland. After dining in company, for example, with a number of bishops and clergy in Carlow, Tocqueville had observed that they appeared to be "clearly as much the heads of a party as the representatives of the church" (episode 12), and several days later, after a long conversation about religion with the bishop of Ossory, William Kinsella, in Kilkenny, he had shrewdly noted, "I believe that he is very sincere in wishing that the church shall not be part of the state, but I wonder if he does not think, at bottom, that the state would do well enough as part of the church" (episode 21).

What Tocqueville thought should be done, however, about moderating the very considerable political power and influence of the Irish clergy, as distinguished from the dangers the clergy posed to the state, is a more difficult question because the answer has more to be inferred from his questions that induced from his observations. He did, however, early indicate that his own mind was still not made up on the question of the "voluntary remuneration" of the Irish clergy when he observed that this proposition would have to be well examined in the light of a "state of affairs altogether particular to Ireland" (episode 14). Tocqueville only then became somewhat more explicit when he asked the Protestant and fanatically anti-Catholic barrister, J. P. Prendergast, in Kilkenny, the leading question, "Do you not think the best way to loosen the ties that unite the people to the clergy would be to give the latter a salary from the state?" (episode 25). When this question is taken in conjunction with several others he also put to Prendergast, it becomes obvious that Tocqueville had, during his six weeks' stay in Ireland, progressively come to view the Irish situation as truly alarming.

"Do you not think," he also asked Prendergast, "if this country separated from England, you would immediately have a violent revolution?" Prendergast replied, of course, that he did not doubt it, and Tocqueville then asked, "Do you think that the temporary dictatorship of England would not be a blessing?"—to which Prendergast agreed. The following day Tocqueville posed the same question, with an interesting gloss, to John George, another Protestant barrister of more Liberal professions. "Do you not think," he asked George, "that a temporary dictatorship exercised in a firm and enlightened manner, like that of Bonaparte after the 18 Brumaire, would be the only way of saving Ireland?" (episode 27). George also agreed, but he then perceptively pointed out that the English party system in the House of Commons was inimical to firm government in Ireland, and more especially when it was at the political mercy of a phalanx of Irish members controlled by O'Connell.

During his visit to Ireland in the summer of 1835, therefore, Tocqueville had come to view the Irish situation as potentially a revolutionary one requiring extraordinary measures and a strong hand. On one side, the inevitable transition from aristocracy to democracy taking place in the western world rendered the pretensions to power of the Irish aristocracy a dangerous political anachronism. On the other, the rude and unenlightened political state of the Irish democracy, led by a clergy with equal political pretensions, made it impossible to entrust it with political power. The only solution, therefore, was that a centralized and enlightened English administration would firmly have to hold the ring in Ireland between the two factions until such time as the legal and traditional privileges of the aristocracy were safely abolished and the nationalist and separatist propensities of the democracy were finally sublimated in a policy of good government and strict justice. The problem of the inordinate political power and influence of the Irish clergy, in the meantime, would have to be resolved by their being paid by the state.

The problem, however, that apparently haunted Tocqueville the most, from the beginning to the end of his Irish journey, was not how political power was to be safely redistributed in Ireland, but rather what was to be done about the all-pervasive problem of poverty. In his early conversation with William Murphy, the wealthy Catholic merchant in Dublin, for example, Tocqueville suggested that perhaps a greater division of landed property in Ireland might allow a larger number of people to live "in greater comfort in the same space" (episode 2). Murphy pointed out that there was really no market in land for small holdings, and that a landlord could hope to realize a good price only by selling his estate as a whole rather than in small parcels. Tocqueville in a marginal note then remarked significantly, "It is the opposite in France. A difference that ought to be well considered." The relationship of the incidence of poverty to the distribution of landed property, however, had been much on Tocqueville's mind since his visit to England in August and September of 1833.

"The state of the poor," Tocqueville had explained on September 7, 1833, "is England's deepest trouble. The number of poor is increasing here at an alarming rate, which in part should be attributed to the defects of the [poor] law."[1] "But the prime and permanent cause of the evil in my opinion," Tocqueville insisted, "is the drastic way in which landed property is not divided up." A year and a half later, shortly before his visit to England and Ireland in 1835, Tocqueville published a *Memoir on Pauperism,* which was the first part of what was to be a two-part study. The occasion for this study apparently was the recently passed Poor Law Amendment Act (1834) in England, more often referred to as the New Poor Law. In this article, after an interesting discussion of the origins, nature, and perceptions of poverty, Tocqueville came down firmly in favor of private charity as the remedy rather than public aid provided by the state in the form of a poor law.[2] In the course of the article, Tocqueville alluded to the problem of the unequal distribution of landed property in England, and in his conclusion remarked that perhaps what was most necessary was not so much the finding of ways to alleviate poverty, but the preventing of it by a more rational redistribution of national wealth.[3]

The awful magnitude of the problem of poverty in Ireland could not only have raised questions in Tocqueville's mind about the efficacy of private charity in alleviating the general misery, but must have deepened his conviction that only a radical redistribution of landed property was capable of preventing it. After his return to France, Tocqueville began to work on the second part of his study on pauperism, which he never completed, but of which his biographer has been able to reconstruct a substantial part.[4] In this unfinished article, Tocqueville proceeded to discuss those remedies, other than private

1. Alexis de Tocqueville, *Oeuvres Complètes* (Paris: Gallimard, 1958), J. P. Mayer, ed., v, 42.

2. Seymour Drescher, *Tocqueville and Beaumont on Social Reform* (New York: Harper & Row, 1968), pp. 1–27.

3. Ibid., p. 13 and p. 26.

4. André Jardin, *Alexis de Tocqueville* (Paris: Hachette littérature, 1984), pp. 233–34.

charity or a poor law, that might provide a solution to the problem of poverty. He began by making a distinction between poverty in the agrarian sector and poverty in the industrial sector; in the case of the former, he proposed the establishment of a peasant proprietary, as had been done in France at the Great Revolution. Whether Tocqueville thought such a radical redistribution of landed property in Ireland would solve the problem of poverty there, given its magnitude, is difficult to say, not only because he apparently did not refer specifically to Ireland in the draft of his article, but also because, when he learned that Beaumont intended to write a book about Ireland, he apparently never wrote another word about that unhappy country.

Whether indeed, on further reflection, Tocqueville modified his views either about what measures England might take in Ireland to effect the peaceful transition from aristocracy to democracy there, or if the Irish clergy should be paid by the English state, must also remain essentially an open question, given the absence of any direct evidence. If Beaumont's study of Ireland, however, which was finally published in 1839, may be taken as a reliable surrogate for Tocqueville's views on Ireland (and there would appear to be some very good circumstantial evidence for doing so)[5] there may be perhaps something more to be said. In his study, Beaumont advocated both a peasant proprietary as a remedy for the problem of poverty and the payment of the Irish clergy by the state as the means for reducing their power and influence with the democracy.[6] Beaumont also recommended that, in effecting the peaceful transition from aristocracy to democracy, England exercise a firm and centralized control in Ireland. "What Ireland needs,"

5. Drescher, pp. 201–17. See, for a very interesting presentation, "Tocqueville and Beaumont: A Rationale for a Collective Study," and particularly p. 212: "After they had almost simultaneously finished the drafts of *Democracy in America* and *L'Irlande* in 1838, Tocqueville insisted that they read each other's works before submitting them, despite special reasons for immediate publication, because it was important that they be fully up to date about each other's ideas, 'in order to be sure that we place ourselves before the public as united in words as we are in hearts.' " Drescher is here quoting a letter from Tocqueville to Beaumont dated November 5, 1838.

6. Gustave de Beaumont, *L'Irlande Sociale, Politique et Religieuse* (Paris: C. Gosselin, 1839). See II, 189–203 for a peasant proprietary, and II, 248–54 for the payment of the clergy by the state.

Beaumont maintained, "is a strong administration, superior to parties, in the shade of which the middle classes might grow, develop, and educate themselves, while the aristocracy would crumble and their remnants disappear."[7] "Here is a great work to be accomplished," he concluded enthusiastically, "the execution of which is offered to the English government."

As great as England's political mission in Ireland might appear to be, however, Beaumont, and presumably Tocqueville, were also convinced that Ireland of herself had an even more significant role to play in the inevitable transformation of the English political system from one ruled by an aristocracy to one governed by a democracy. Because the imperatives of empire would never allow England to concede Ireland a separate or independent political existence, and because the democracy in Ireland would soon triumph over the patently bankrupt aristocracy there, the English political system must also be leavened eventually by the Irish democracy in favor of the English democracy. The chief ingredient in that yeasting process would prove to be those radical Irish members elected to Parliament.[8] For Beaumont and Tocqueville, therefore, democracy was as inevitable in England as it was in Ireland. The supreme historical irony, however, was that England, by having to deny Ireland its national freedom in the interest of her own imperial greatness, was destined to achieve, sooner rather than later, that basic social equality that was the inevitable concomitant of the triumph of democracy.

7. Ibid., II, 183.
8. Ibid., II, 325–57.

Note on the Text

Tocqueville's account of his Irish experiences, as presented in this volume, consists of forty-seven discrete episodes, or sections, of varying nature and length. They include, for example, brief notes (8), comments (6), descriptions (12), interviews (8), conversations (11), and essays (2), and range from fewer than 100 words to more than 6000. Sometimes Tocqueville wrote his account of these episodes the same day they took place, but more often, apparently, he composed them several days later when he had had a little more time to reflect. Tocqueville nearly always gave his Irish manuscripts the date when the episode actually occurred and not when he composed his account of it. The forty-seven episodes presented here, therefore, have been arranged in chronological order according to their occurrence. Only three of the forty-seven episodes (numbers 2, 32, and 44) have not been dated according to their occurrence, and each requires some particular explanation with regard to its chronology and its place in the presentation here.

In episode 2 (Tocqueville's conversation with William Murphy) the manuscript is not dated. The conversation probably occurred during Tocqueville's initial stay in Dublin (July 6–17), if not indeed in London (May 8–June 24) before his arrival in Ireland. I have arbitrarily placed it at the beginning of Tocqueville's sojourn in Dublin because of the general nature of its content, dealing as it does with poverty and unemployment and their possible amelioration through a poor law or by better use or distribution of land. Episode 32, on the other hand, describing in detail a visit to Muckross Abbey, is simple to date because there is a note in the Beaumont papers of their visit to Killarney dated July 30, 1835. He arrived in Cork city from Kilkenny (92 miles) on the evening of July 27, and apparently spent the next day there. He set out for Killarney (54 miles) the following morning, July 29, and arrived there that afternoon. He, therefore, probably visited Muckross Abbey and the Lakes the next day, July 30, and then set out for Limerick (69 miles) the following day, July 31, where he expected to pick up his mail, and spent the night there. The next morning, August 1, as may be seen in episode

33, he left Limerick for Galway (65 miles), via Ennis, where he arrived that evening.

It is episode 44, however, that provides the most difficult problems with regard to chronology. In some of his longer episodes, some nine in fact, Tocqueville provided a title page. On that page he entitled the episode and usually dated it. When he began the account of the episode proper on the first page he usually entitled and dated it again. On the title page of episode 44, however, he entitled the episode, but added, by way of dating it, "begun at Cork, July 28, 1835." On the first page of the episode, contrary to his usual practice, there is no title or date, and in the first paragraph, moreover, he announces that on arriving in Tuam in the province of Connaught, he proceeded to read the addresses of his letters of introduction. The problem, of course, is that he did not arrive in Tuam, as may be seen in episode 42, until August 4, and if he did begin this episode (44) on July 28, he got no further than the title page. To complicate matters even further, this episode is internally dated as taking place on a Saturday and Sunday, while the narrative has it also taking place on the afternoon and evening, and following morning, of his arrival in Tuam on August 4, which were a Tuesday and a Wednesday. Given the intractability of the various chronologies, the problem of dating the actual occurrence of this episode would appear to be impossible to resolve.

Logically, the episode cannot have been written before the last verifiable fact in it (in terms of time) had taken place. That fact is, Tocqueville arrived about noon in Tuam from Galway city (about 21 miles) on August 4. Whether indeed Tocqueville continued on to Castlebar (about 36 miles) that afternoon, or actually visited a priest and minister near Tuam that Tuesday evening and following Wednesday morning, and then went on to Castlebar that afternoon, August 5, will probably never be resolved. The internal evidence in this episode, however, also raises another possibility—that this episode *actually* never took place in its integrity, but is *really* a montage, or composite "set-piece" that is morally rather than historically true. In other words, it is really a moral tale or essay based on a series of actual events. There is no doubt that the comparison of the priest and minister had been on Tocqueville's mind since he wrote to his cousin, the Countess Grancey, on July 26. The "democratic tirade" of William Kinsella, the bishop of Ossory, that same evening at dinner, denouncing the cruelty of landlords in general and the marquis of Sligo in particular (whose tenants' charity was all that stood between the poor and starvation, and whose dogs were even better fed than his starving tenants) has also been incorporated by Tocqueville into this long episode comparing the priest and the minister. Finally, on his way from Carlow to Waterford, in episode 17, he noticed at Jerpoint Abbey near Thomastown, in County Kilkenny, the touching attachment of the people to their religious beliefs in wanting to bury their dead around the ruined walls in consecrated ground, and again he underlines the same point on July 30, in his Muckross Abbey episode, before finally incorporating the theme in his priest and minister episode. Tocqueville chose to write a moral rather than a historical essay in this comparative episode probably to avoid libeling the actual Protestant minister (who would be juxtaposed to the Catholic priest) and thus imposing on the hospitality, however slight, of the minister, and especially on the confidence of those who had written letters of introduction for Tocqueville to him. Because the nature of this episode will not allow it to be dated in its historical time, it has been placed in the chronological sequence of episodes in terms of when it was thought to be written. The episode was probably written on the afternoon or evening of August 4 when Tocqueville visited Tuam; or, if he did not stay in Tuam and continued on to Castlebar that day, it was most likely written the next day, August 5, in Castlebar.

Finally a word must be said about the manuscript, and how Tocqueville approached his writing. Tocqueville's method in working was to take sheets of paper, of about 7 1/2 by 12 inches, fold them in half, and then cut them to produce sheets of about 6 by 7 1/2 inches. He then folded these sheets in half lengthwise, to provide a left and a right half of the sheet of paper. He wrote in black ink and usually entitled and dated his episode at the top of the left-hand side of the page, and then began his account of the episode at the top of the right half, reserving the rest of the left-hand side for footnotes, comments, and any additions and corrections he might care to make.

He then turned the page over and continued his account on the other side in the same way. If the account of the episode extended to more than the front and back of the first page, he numbered the second page in the upper left-hand corner, and so on, if more pages were necessary. He usually indicated the end of an episode, or sometimes a significant part within it, by a short heavy line. His rules for capitalization and punctuation were highly idiosyncratic. He did not capitalize the words at the beginning of sentences, and he appears to have had no rule with regard to the capitalization of proper nouns. He generally used commas instead of periods, and often forgot to put a question mark at the end of an interrogative. The capitalization and punctuation, therefore, have been made to conform with modern usage in the interest of making the text more readable.

Note on the Map

In 1835 the mail coaches traveling between the major towns in Ireland averaged about eight miles an hour. Tocqueville and Beaumont departed Dublin for their tour of the South and West of Ireland on July 18 or 19, and arrived in Carlow, a distance of 46 miles, on the afternoon or evening of Sunday, July 19. The two travelers left Carlow for Waterford, 45 miles away, two days later on July 21. They remained in Waterford attending the assizes for two days, and on July 24 they departed for Kilkenny, a distance of 30 miles. After attending the assizes in Kilkenny for two days, they set out for Cork, 92 miles, early on the morning of July 27. They arrived in Cork that evening and remained there the following day. The next day, July 29, they apparently departed for Killarney, a distance of some 54 miles. It is not entirely clear which route they took to Killarney, but in all likelihood they chose the shorter route, by Macroom, rather than going by Millstreet. They remained in Killarney sightseeing the next day, July 30, and the following day they left for Limerick via Newcastle West, a distance of 69 miles. Early the next morning, August 1, they set out for Galway, 65 miles distant, and arrived there that evening. They remained in Galway sightseeing and attending the assizes for two days, and then on August 4, they left for Castlebar, a distance of 57 miles. They spent the next day in Castlebar, and the following morning, August 6, they departed for Newport-Pratt, 11 miles away. They returned to Castlebar on August 8, and must have left almost immediately for Dublin, a distance of 144 miles. In all likelihood they broke their journey in Longford that night and arrived late the next evening, Sunday, August 9, in Dublin. In all, the two travelers covered 624 miles in 22 days in their circuit of the South and West of Ireland. This map of Irish roads in 1837 was originally produced as Plate I in the atlas accompanying the "Second Report of the Railway Commissioners, Ireland, 1838," and has been reproduced in T. W. Freeman, *Pre-Famine Ireland: A Study in Historical Geography* (Manchester, 1957), p. 110.

Index